MW00437271

ORGANIZE
A S Y O U G O

ORGANIZE

A S Y O U G O

Successful Skills for Busy Lifestyles

M a r i e R i c k s

First edition.

Cover design by Marie Calder Ricks.
Cover photos and copyright page
artwork by Thomas E. Ricks,
www.tomricks.com.

Also visit *www.houseoforder.com* for more
information regarding your organization needs,
to purchase organization products, schedule
a personal consultation, speaking engagement,
or educational seminar.

Organize As You Go

Copyright © 2009 by Marie Calder Ricks.
Printed and bound in the United State of America.
All rights reserved. No part of this book may be
reproduced in any form or by any electronic or
mechanical means including information storage
and retrieval systems without permission in
writing from publisher, except by a reviewer,
who may quote brief passages in a review.
Published by Marie Calder Ricks, 6756 West
10050 North, Highland, Utah 84003.

ISBN 13 978-0-9788579-4-3
ISBN-10 0-9788579-4-1

*This book was written, with all my love and
encouragement, to anyone desiring
more order in his or her busy life.*

*Improved personal organization can be a
lifetime gift for you and all those
within your influence.
May you gain the skills to change
for the better!*

Contents

Acknowledgments..xi
Introduction..1

Organized Every Day

1 Ten Minutes a Day Keeps Disorder Away...7
2 Get Ready for the Day 9
3 The Slinky Principle 11
4 Do What Will Stay Done 13
5 Personal Speed Limits 15
6 Slow Life Down 17
7 Time for Little Things...20
8 New Habits for Forever 22

An Organized Home

 9 Ninety-Minute Miracles..27
10 Prune Back Personal Possessions 30
11 Redefine Refrigerator Organization..32
12 Regularly Replenish..34
13 A Functional Home Filing System 36
14 Your Password Cracker 38
15 Take Control of Endless Emails..41
16 Organize Digital Photos..44

Organization Challenges

17 Organization Monsters.. 51
18 From Frazzled and Frustrated to Focused 53
19 Think It Through 55
20 Deal with Double Discouragements 57
21 Change the Unchangeable... 59
22 Withdraw, Regroup and Reemerge....................................... 61
23 Time to Catch Up 63
24 Confront Personal Confusion 65
25 Bad News to Good Progress 68
26 Transition Times 71
27 Stop Before You're Tired 73

Organization for Parents and Children

28 Do the Worst Jobs First 79
29 The Oops Syndrome... 81
30 Teach Others to Wait.. 84
31 Summer Chores for Children 86
32 Tell, Teach, Time, and Self-Initiative 89
33 Warm Weather Clothing Standards....................................... 92
34 Summer Stress and a September List.................................... 95
35 Regroup When They Get Grumpy.. 98
36 Teach Children Not to Hit... 101
37 The Power of Nurturing.. 104
38 The Answer Is No.. 106

Organized for Big Events and Holidays

39 Organize for the Holidays 111
40 Finish Up and Move Forward 114
41 Have Backup Plans... 116
42 A Thanks Bank Perspective 118
43 The Angel on Your Street 121
44 Maintain Functional Chaos 123
45 Catnap Craze.. 125
46 The Day After 127
47 Shed and Share New Stuff 129

Organized for Traveling and Moving

48 Your Motel Stay 133
49 The Big Move... 136
50 Urban Camping in a New Abode.................................. 138
51 Finish the Move.. 140

Organized for the Future

52 Weekly Maps 145
53 Map out Twenty Years... 149

Endnote... 154
Biography 155
Also by Marie Ricks... 156

Acknowledgments

Writing a book is not an isolated experience. Your family, associates, and clients all contribute, either consciously or unknowingly, for they influence your thinking and eventually share their wisdom through the book you write.

Having said that, I would like to specifically thank the experts in my immediate circle: Jennifer Ricks for acting as my editor, Brian Ricks for his technical contributions, Tom Ricks for his artistic expertise, David Ricks for his long-distance encouragement, and Tyler Ricks for his professional advice. Lastly, Jim, my husband, mentored me on a daily basis. How can anyone not succeed with such consistent support?

To those of you who have shared your experiences as you have written from around the world about the growing and changing that has happened as you have practiced new organization skills, I also say my thank you. My professional peers, students, and attendees at my presentations have taught me, too.

Without you, this book would be less. With you, others can learn and grow towards better and happier lives, all because they, too, learned how to organize as they go!

Introduction

The premise of *Organize As You Go* is that most people have little or no time to stop and get organized. But, if you can be organized even as you take care of personal needs, familial nurturing, and professional responsibilities, you can also find the time to enjoy life and smell the roses, as it were.

Getting just ten percent more organized will give you an additional ninety minutes in every day. This significant amount of time will allow you to enjoy life more and to achieve the personal dreams you so desire. It is in small shifts in behavior, new habits, and strong leadership that organization improvements are best established.

As you may know, I am a professional organizer who writes books, teaches classes, and presents in various venues. I love the adventure and challenge of discovering more organized ways to conduct my own life, in addition to helping others find answers to their specific needs.

Life is constantly stretching and challenging all my organization skills. Memories of simple days seem far away, and I'm always wondering what tomorrow with drop in my path. I'm here and I'm there. I am off and gone first thing in the morning one day and then am home without outside commitments the next. Often external responsibilities seem to overlap with my immediate family's needs. There are people constantly seeking my time and needing me right away.

The concept of *organizing as you go* means bringing all projects to the next beginning point before you stop and completely finishing whenever you can. It means watching for holes in your habits so that you close cupboard doors before you leave a room and tighten the handle of a leaky tap (with plans to repair it this weekend)—thus fixing problems as you go. It means that you can find more in order in your home, desk, and office more often.

For myself, I'm trying more than ever to empty my car right after running errands and restock it with the supplies I need for my next trip around and about. I'm trying to have extra makeup on hand so I'm not scraping the bottom of a lipstick tube in order to look pretty in the morning. I'm making sure that if a shirt needs mending, it is put in my sewing closet and then repaired as a priority.

I'm going just a bit slower and doing just a bit more to keep order in my busy life. I'm not leaving the kitchen until the dishes are rinsed and in the dishwasher. I'm trying to transfer my scribbles from post-it notes to permanent places right after phone conversations. I'm emptying my purse of receipts and trash every time I do the weekly budget. On Mondays, I'm putting all the canned fruit and frozen meats I will need for the upcoming week in the refrigerator so my meal preparations will be easier because the meat will be thawed and the fruit chilled when I fix dinner.

In your daily routines, where could you use these skills to better organize as you go? With just a bit of practice, a little bit of initial inconvenience, and a few moments of time, you will find your efficiency and effectiveness will increase considerably as you organize as you go.

Because each of us is learning and growing in our organization capacities in our various busy seasons of life, I am constantly trying to discover and apply new skills to become, and stay, more organized. More and more, I find success by organizing as I go. This book is the compilation of my favorite organization skills learned through experience during the past several years. I hope that each and every chapter will have an impact on your life and that you will find answers to problems that face you at home, work, and in other capacities. Indeed, the skills in this book can help you keep up with the varying needs of every season and help you gain more control.

May you implement better organization skills and then spread the good news to all your busy friends. It takes a lot of work to be organized, but it takes a lot more work to be disorganized!

~ Marie

ORGANIZED
EVERY DAY

1

Ten Minutes a Day Keeps Disorder Away

I spend a lot of my time helping others find order in their lives. Sometimes it is cleaning up, sometimes it is cleaning out, and often it is finding the reasons behind the mess in the first place as we both clean out and clean up.

No matter the reasons, the situation, or the circumstances, I have found that anyone who devotes ten minutes at a time to bringing their life back to order will make tremendous progress. Using a timer can make it a game. Whether it is getting the front room looking nice  enough for company, getting the dishes cleaned and in the cupboard, or getting the laundry folded and put away, spending an extra ten minutes focusing on home management may be all you need to obtain the order you desire.

Ten minutes lasts a long time when I am cleaning up and out. It's no fun, it makes me sweaty, and it is seemingly thankless.

But with the timer set and a determination not to be detoured by the phone, TV, or a knock on the door, I can keep disorder at bay in my life. The newspapers get tossed, the blanket on the back of the couch gets folded, and the crumbs under the kitchen table are finally swept up.

You can try this new habit today. Set the timer for ten minutes and go to work. Ruthlessly discard unneeded items, make stacks of things to go elsewhere, and start gaining control again. Work hard, stay focused, and keep at it until the timer dings. For me, it is easier to spend this ten minutes earlier in the day, as afternoon and evening hours seem to slip by with other priorities.

After you have established this ten minutes a day habit for yourself, engage your family members' help. Work with pre-school children during the day and older children when they are home. Have a clean-up session together before lunch, another before dinner, and lastly one session before bedtime. By modeling to your children that ten minutes a day keeps disorder away, you can both make your home orderly now and ensure the probability your children will grow up to be more organized. Bring your home to a place of order each and every day to sleep better, live better, and keep disorder at bay.

2

Get Ready for the Day

There are core morning activities every child, teenager, and adult should routinely do to appropriately get ready for the day. These simple but repetitive habits will lay a solid foundation for you, your spouse, and your children whether in the midst of a heavy school schedule or in the leisure of summer days. Encourage your children to get ready for the day before they are allowed to watch cartoons, play with their toys, or start a personal project.

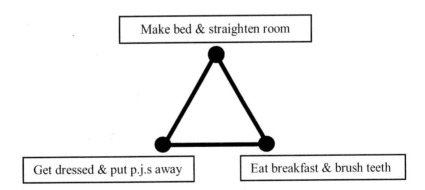

Except on rare and special occasions, every family member should make his or her bed and straighten up their bedroom as the first core activity. Second, they should get dressed and put their pajamas away. Third, they should have breakfast, clean up after themselves, and brush their teeth.

With young children you might use the shape of a triangle indicating that each point represents a different morning responsibility.

Take a look at the morning routines of your family. Consistency in good morning habits on a day-to-day basis will lay the foundation for order in your lives so teach your family to get ready for the day before doing anything else. Then, motivate family members according to their level of maturity, as in these examples:

"If you get ready for the day, then you may watch morning cartoons."

"If you get ready for the day, then you may play with your toys or video games."

"If you get ready for the day, then you may get out your craft project and work on it until lunchtime."

Getting themselves ready for the day will help family members actively participate in ordering their private lives and contribute significantly to the order in your home. As you practice with them, you will find a day started out right has much more of a chance to end right, too.

3

The Slinky Principle

It is true, and sometimes discouraging, that work is anything that stops being fun before it gets done. However, your work can get done for today, can be finished for this week, and can be completed until next month. In order to move from *never done* to *I'm done (for now)*, you must understand and employ the slinky principle.

A slinky is a rounded piece of metal that is produced as a continuous spring. Children often put it at the top of the stairs and watch it spring over itself and go down the stairs one at a time.

For organization purposes, the slinky represents your unending work. Over and over again, there's a pile of laundry, a sink full of dishes, and a dirty bathroom all demanding your attention.

If you draw a line with a permanent marking pen down one side of the slinky, you have start and stop places all along the slinky. You can approach personal and home organization in this same way. Here are some examples of the slinky principle:

"I will do two loads of laundry each week day, which will allow me to keep up on my family's needs. With two loads completed, the laundry can be done for today!"

"I will do the dishes immediately after dinner and empty the dishwasher before leaving for work in the morning. Then the dishes will be done for today."

"I will clean the upstairs bathroom on Saturday mornings and let my teenage boys clean their downstairs bath when they do their weekly chores. Then the bathrooms will be cleaned for the week."

Ask yourself what slinky jobs are burdensome to you right now and how you can finish them for a day, a week, or a month so you can stop having those heavy undones on your mind. May you understand and employ the slinky principle with success. Lots of your responsibilities won't ever be done, but they can be finished for now.

4

Do What Will Stay Done

Whether you are in a time of great stress and challenge or you are dealing with the mundane routines of raising a family or keeping a steady job, finishing small projects from your to-do list that will stay done for awhile will help you stay organized and give you a sense of control.

As you look at your daunting to-do list, deal with the items that once done will "stay done" for a while. These items aren't necessarily very important and probably would normally never make it to the top of your list, but tackling these items will give you some quick and lasting satisfaction.

For example, take several minutes while you are talking to your friend on the phone to clean out the kitchen junk drawer, or match up the winter gloves in the coat closet while waiting for the children to come home from the bus. Vanquish the cobwebs on the ceiling of your bathroom. Go through your underwear and discard unused items. Throw away all the dried-up pens in your home office desk.

Try to do something every day that will stay done for a little while. This simple habit brings a certain sense of accomplishment that makes it easier to go back to other repetitive and mundane tasks.

Especially on bad, stressful days, review your to-do list and find quick items you can do that will stay done for a while. Even when you are not thinking well because of stress, you can complete these useful projects so they don't stack up. Learning to tackle small projects in the midst of your everyday responsibilities, especially if those projects will stay done for a while, will bring a sense of control and comfort.

5

Personal Speed Limits

Have you ever received a speeding ticket? You were driving somewhere totally absorbed in yourself and your pressures, when you see sirens in your rear view mirror and realize that you might have been going too fast.

Another kind of speeding often happens in your daily life. You try to keep up with the speed of the needs around you. You go faster and faster and get less and less sleep. Your life is spinning around and you feel out of control.

Much as speed limit signs keep a road safe for all drivers, personal speed limits help you keep a safer life pace.

There are three personal speed limits that significantly improve your capacity to function in an organized manner: sufficient sleep, proper eating habits, and appropriate stress management. Ignoring these limits always results in a speeding ticket—not the kind of speeding ticket that costs money, but the kind that takes away energy, perspective, and functionality.

Surpassing the limits of sufficient sleep, proper eating, and appropriate stress management will give you a "ticket." You can outwit a ticket here and you can avoid a ticket there because your body policeman might be otherwise occupied, but eventually all of those violations will catch up with you and land you sick in bed.

Take time to review your personal speed limits and set some goals. For example:

"I will be in bed by _____ each weekday night and by ___ on the weekends even when our company is here."

"I will leave time before and after all my projects, commitments, and activities for setup and cleanup so I can stay in charge of my stress. Sometimes I will say *'no'* or *'later'* or maybe even *'I will have to think about that for a bit'* before making further commitments."

"I will eat treats that I enjoy, but I will only have ___ bites before I push the plate back, put the dish in the fridge, or dump the rest down the disposal."

Especially during times of fun, friends, and frolic it pays to drive safely from beginning to end. Review your own personal speed limits. Decide what your limits will be and how you will handle your food consumption, your sleeping habits, and your stress—without any tickets at all!

6

Slow Life Down

In addition to applying personal speed limits, there is another skill that will help you feel more in control of your life. This is especially true if you have been in a hurry for several consecutive weeks as your commitments have stacked themselves one upon another without relief and you have too many people to keep happy all at once. As your schedule tightens, you might notice that your joy begins to diminish because hurrying doesn't allow you enough time and space to enjoy the small pleasures of each day.

If you are always worrying about being on time, finishing up the dishes, remembering to put everything in your vehicle, and being upset with the kids because they are so slow, life loses its treasures.

There are answers to help you enjoy life again, to actually see the budding daffodils at the park and hear the birds chirping in the trees. Modify your schedule just slightly so you can walk slower, drive slower, and talk slower. By doing this, your tension will dissipate, your spirits will rise, and your mood will significantly improve.

Imagine what your family and/or coworkers will think when you walk unhurriedly into the room, smiling with assurance, and then proceed with a confident, but leisurely, gait? All this is possible if you can be just a little bit early, start a little sooner, and have things more in order as you proceed on your way.

During the next few days, watch your own routines and look for ways and places where you can slow down occasionally to treasure up the precious moments. For example, when your children climb into the car after school, surprise them by sitting completely still for a just a moment before starting up the engine and saying, "Did you notice that the sky is particularly bright blue today?" Then, start up the car and be on your way. When you are finishing the final touches for an evening out, walk up to your spouse and just look at him or her for a minute before offering a short, graceful compliment. "Honey, did you know I have always liked the color of your eyes?" The whole evening will be more interesting because you slowed down just long enough. When you awake in the morning, lie in bed just for a moment and feel the sheets, notice the pattern of the shadows on your ceiling, and then jump up to attend to your responsibilities. A few moments of being in charge makes a big difference between feeling confident and calm instead of rushed and out of control.

Rearranging the order in which you accomplish certain tasks also allows you to slow it down and remove the rushed feeling from your schedule. For example, decide what you will wear the night before so there is time to look for sagging hems, loose buttons and broken zippers before the pressure to dress and get off the next day. Get up a few minutes earlier than usual, which will allow time for dealing with morning squabbles in a more controlled and calm manner because you have a few minutes to spare. Or, put the kids' lunches together the night before so in the few precious morning moments there is time to hug and kiss them twice as you hand them their sacks. Find other, simple ways to slow it down during the important moments of your day by rearranging your schedule.

As you incorporate these *slow-it-down* skills, you will have time to smell the yellow rosebuds in your front yard, watch a hawk land while you wait at a stop light, and smile at the sunrise as you drop the children off for school.

Everything can be different. Going a bit slower on purpose and taking some of the hurry out of your life will indeed make a significant difference in your personal patience and private joys.

7

Time for Little Things

As you prioritize and make sure you attend to the big, important responsibilities and consistently work on your never-ending to do list, you might leave the little things for later—much later. Because they are little things that often don't even make it to your to do list, they can remain undone for a bit and really not undo your life, but eventually you start living a slightly frayed life because you don't regularly take a few minutes each day for little things.

 Look for the little things that need doing in your life. Give yourself permission to turn from the bigger responsibilities while dinner is cooking to update your makeup kit, reattach the carpet edge on your staircase, clean out the glove compartment, or do something else you have let go for some time. Mend your sweater. Tighten the loose screw on the kitchen cupboard. Pump up the flat bike tire. Answer the difficult email.

Trim your frayed life back just a bit and come to a place of greater order, all in a few minutes each day.

This means no more cobwebs on your front porch, a clean purse, mended garden gloves, and on and on. Why live with so many undone little things?

Give yourself permission to finish up, clean up, and mend the little things so you can enjoy life's best moments. For a just few minutes each day, look for the little things and attend to them before they become bigger, more dangerous and time-consuming problems.

8

New Habits for Forever

New habits come slowly, but they can last a lifetime. Creating new habits is hard. Most of us have very ingrained routines that are hard to change. We get discouraged and frustrated, and we want to give up. It sometimes seems easier not to change, but that is not true.

Because change is a slow process, try to focus on only one to three goals at once.

Here is an example: One of your goals is to serve more nutritious meals to your family. At first you want to make every meal perfectly nutritious during the upcoming month, but this is too much to do at once. If you try to tackle too much at once, failure is inevitable!

Try to define your goals in more specific terms that are easier to tackle; take one step at a time. Maybe start with a goal to serve nutritious dinners for one week. Prepare a Master Menu plan on Monday morning. You only need seven ideas per week, a number you can handle for your one-week goal. Keep your goal in mind when you do your grocery shopping for the week and plan plenty of time for meal preparation each afternoon.

You might need to write goal prompts in your planner to remind you to give yourself enough time to shop and cook in order to meet your nutritious dinners' goal. Keep focused on success. Written reminders are helpful, especially until the habit is firmly planted into your routine.

After you finish a week at your new goal, take some time before the next week starts to think through the roadblocks to your success. What went right? What went wrong? What other habits do you need to change in order to eventually meet your ultimate goal? For example, when you have thawed meat in the refrigerator, it is easier to put together meals. Next week you could try to consistently thaw the meat you need in advance. Maybe it would be better for you to buy pre-peeled carrots because you never find time to peel full carrots. Maybe you hated cleaning up the kitchen after the meal, so next week you'll try to clean up as much as possible while you're waiting for the family to gather before the meal. Make new written reminders to help you with your new goals.

What new habits would you like to have? You can use these same techniques with any new goals for which you are striving. Focus on specific, step-by-step goals that will lead you to your ultimate goal. Use written reminders to keep you on track so one experience builds upon another. Resolve roadblocks and add new goals to keep you headed towards success.

Initially, you may make only small amounts of progress, but eventually attaining your goals will make your life easier and you and your family happier. When you have attained one small goal, look for new steps you can take to reach your ultimate goal.

Step by step, you can find success as you establish new habits.

AN
ORGANIZED
HOME

9

Ninety-Minute Miracles

Have you tried a ninety-minute miracle? So many times when I personally coach, people struggle with where to start, what to do, and how to incorporate the best methods in the daily maintenance of their home, garage, and yard. While these are important questions, the real challenge for them, and for most of us, is simply getting to work.

Many people want to change, they want to do things differently. They want clean up their desk, organize the kitchen drawers, or reorganize the laundry room shelves. But tackling a mess is very difficult and so they never quite get to it. Change, however, can be made easier with consistent forward progress.

There is nothing like setting a timer for ninety minutes and organizing with a focused goal. If you do that every day for a week, you will find that your personal environment, home, and office desk will become more organized simply because you *got to it.*

As much as having the right methods, making proper decisions, and obtaining the best tools, simply getting going is what needs doing. I visited a home recently and helped a friend who was momentarily disabled with back problems. Her kitchen was a real mess so I worked with her home-schooled children clearing off the top of the refrigerator, soaking the dirty dishes, and cleaning up the kitchen counters. We swept and scrubbed the kitchen floor, finished up the dishes, started dinner, and even polished the kitchen table. Ninety minutes later we were all astounded at how much was accomplished.

I encourage you and your family to have a ninety-minute miracle time, where you each organize something. If they are older and capable, have them clean up the bookcases, tackle the bedroom messes, or work with those stacks of unruly boxes in the garage. Let everyone who can participate have an assignment. If there are younger family members, work in teams of two (one older and one younger) and clean up a storage area, the family room, or even a linen closet. A ninety-minute timer can make a difference, because it will get everyone moving, get something accomplished, and bring improvement, change, and even seeming miracles.

Remember, you will need robust boxes or sturdy plastic bags for sorting and a larger working surface upon which to work. Label the sorting containers: *give away*, *put away elsewhere*, and *toss*. You will also need a clear direction as to how much you want to keep and how much you should discard or share. In my coaching experience, most people can get rid of half of everything they own and not really miss their lesser treasures. Work with that goal in mind. Lastly, focus your energy to bring this particular project to a reasonable finish within the ninety-minute period.

So, for example, you decide to clean out a storage room. Set up a table as your working surface. Find large bags or boxes, label them, and place them on the perimeter of the table. Bring the first box to sort through to the table, open it, and begin making decisions. Continue to work until the timer dings ninety minutes later. Leave the table and sorting containers set up, shut the storage room door and return to regular life. Tomorrow you can return to your ninety-miracle project again. Oh, the feeling of accomplishment to finally be getting to some of the messes in your life and conquering them.

In the middle of the flurry of your current activities, with all the other challenges and commitments that you have, choose an organization project, set a timer, take ninety minutes, and work on that specific need. Watch the miracles of organization began to happen with renewed possibility in your life.

10

Prune Back
Personal Possessions

Spring is the time of year when pruning the bushes and trees in your yard can be a part of your annual routine. Time consuming and frustrating as this pruning can be, it provides long-term benefits that outweigh the inconvenience. I've discovered that three pruning principles—trim off, thin back, and discard—apply to my life in general, not just to the landscape plants in my yard.

When pruning a tree, you trim off dead branches. Using this same principle, cut off, cut out, and get rid of unneeded, lifeless items in your home. As you prune around the house, look for things that are outdated, don't work, or you don't like anymore and then clip them out.

Second, when pruning a tree, you also thin out some of the useful branches so other branches have a place to grow. Once the unneeded items are pruned from your home, consider additional thinning. For example, you bought those red pillows thinking they would look so nice in the living room, but they have never really matched and are now stuffed in the closet. Its time they were thinned out. Get rid of those pants you bought on sale and have never used. Recycle the extra grocery store bags cluttering your pantry. Remember that a little less of everything will free up a lot of space needs and simplify everything. Thinning will ease your routines and give you more time and capacity because there will be less mess.

Finally, when you prune, you have to gather and discard your trimmings. This is the last and most essential part of pruning your home. Many times, if you only get the pruned items out to the car but not to the dump or thrift store, someone will find them and begin to ask questions.

"Oh no, what are you doing? Why are you giving that away? How can you do this with our treasures?"

So to avoid trouble, gather up your trimmings and make sure the purging is complete!

It's time to prune around your house. First trim off the dead branches—anything that is no longer functional. Second, thin out so there will be room for later growth. Finally, finish this pruning project with a trip to the trash, the dump, or the charity store.

Pruning your personal possessions will relieve you of stress, keep your environment clean and pleasing, and make you feel re-energized for new projects and activities.

11

Redefine Refrigerator Organization

Keeping your refrigerator organized will change your life! It's easy for your refrigerator to become chaotic because several people use it without much thought of organization. However, there are several things that you can do to keep the refrigerator more organized and workable.

Establish standard places where you keep food that is always in the refrigerator such as milk, eggs, meats, fresh vegetables, fresh fruits, and proteins (which includes cheeses, yogurts and deli meats). You might put milk, meats, and eggs on shelves and vegetables, fruits, and protein items such as string cheese and hot dogs in drawers.

Keep like items with like items—all the condiments together, all the produce together, and all the cold drinks together. You might also consider putting condiments in a larger container so on hot dog night you can pull them all out in one trip.

Think carefully about what to keep in the door of your refrigerator. This should be a place for items you pull from this appliance frequently such as milk, soft drinks, margarine, and sack lunches. Sometimes these door shelves will be empty because things will be coming in and out, especially if the door is used for sack lunches. Try not to crowd this space with things you rarely use, like those exotic pickles and maraschino cherries. The door is a convenient area of the refrigerator and should be reserved for frequently used items.

After establishing standard places for your most common foods, designate two shelves (or parts of shelves), one for *eat all you want* and a second for *don't touch*. Teach your family members that one shelf means *have at it* and another means *please don't touch, this is tonight's dinner*.

When you refill your refrigerator after you go grocery shopping, remember to put new behind old. This keeps the milk fresh and helps keep everybody happy when it's time for cold cereal in the morning. Putting old behind new also keeps the eggs rotated, the yogurts fresh, and the produce as crisp as possible.

Once you have your refrigerator organized, consider clearing it out regularly, maybe every Saturday evening, as part of your preparations for dinner. This will keep mold and bad smells at bay. In addition to offering leftovers from the frig for dinner, serve some kind of easy-to-prepare dish to fill out the meal such as fried, scrambled, or boiled eggs.

Finally, just before you go grocery shopping, when your refrigerator is mostly empty, wipe down the outside of the refrigerator and each interior shelf. Implementing these simple habits will help the refrigerator serve instead of worry you.

12

Regularly Replenish

How would you like to never run out of anything anymore—gas, batteries, prescriptions—nothing? The habit of regularly replenishing saves time, trouble, and hassle. The following four concepts will help you keep ahead and well stocked.

First, set earlier refill standards. When I talk to people and ask them how low they let the gas get in their car before they get uptight, I get a variety of answers.

"Well, I have a gas can in the back if I need to walk to a station."

"I wait till the red light goes on."

"Well, I don't notice much until I'm close to driving on fumes."

By setting an earlier refill standard, you will always have gas. As soon as the gas gauge hits the one-quarter mark, plan on looking for a gas station. This gives you a couple of days to be near your regular station. It is just a small, but important change in habit. If you're always one quarter of the way full, you will never run out of gas. This same concept applies to keeping fresh milk in the frig by buying enough each shopping trip to last past the next anticipated shopping day. It means adding catsup to the grocery list when you pull the last catsup bottle from the pantry. It means getting new disposable diapers when you open the last box, not when you pull the last fresh diaper out of that same box.

The second concept that will help you regularly replenish is keeping written reminders. When you fill a prescription, write a reminder on your calendar several days before you need to refill the prescription again. Give yourself enough time to call in and pick up the prescription before you completely run out of medication.

The third concept is keeping an extra set. You use batteries for your cell phone, laptop, camera, and more. Always have a second, fresh set of batteries for every type you regularly use. If you buy a new camera, get two sets of rechargeable batteries, and have one of them charging so that they will be ready at a moment's notice. Do the same with your laptop and any other item that needs fresh batteries occasionally. With your cell phone, have a regular habit for recharging at a certain time.

Fourth, prepare for the next time this time. For example, as you come home from running errands today, clean out your car. Make sure you have a stash of extra change, full water bottles, and a supply of emergency cereal for your young children. The next time you climb in your car, you probably won't even be thinking about some of these needs, but you will be safe because at the end of the last trip you replenished for the next time.

During the next few days, find one or two places where you could really improve your replenishing habits by refilling earlier, using written notes, keeping spares, and preparing this time for next time.

13

A Functional Home Filing System

So much of the modern world is focused on electronics. We have cell phones, email, and online everything—all of which claims to cut down on paper use. But if your home is like many, there's paper everywhere—unopened mail on the entryway table, phone numbers and policy pamphlets stacked near the phone, bills and invoices scattered over the desk, ticket stubs and photos pinned on the bulletin board.

Too many papers can be overwhelming and oppressive. As a home manager, you need to establish an effective way to handle paperwork by setting up a home office with tools, supplies, and a workable filing system.

First, gather or purchase file folders to help you manage the inflow and outgo of paperwork. To start, purchase about one hundred manila file folders in a three-tab format and one hundred hanging file folders. Also, purchase labels that will fit on the tabs of the manila file folders so you can use the folders again and again as your needs change. You will also need some marking pens, a stack of index cards, and a sturdy hanging file folder drawer or box.

Next, gather the paperwork that has accumulated around the house. Begin sorting this stack on a large, clean surface, usually a counter or table. Using index cards, label the piles as you make them. For example, you might label an index card *Home Insurance* and put this card next to the stack of home insurance papers. You might label another stack *To Scrapbook* and a third *Tax Documents*. As your piles multiply, you can keep track of what paperwork belongs where. If your stacks get too big, feel free to divide them into two smaller, and more specifically labeled, stacks.

Use wording that works for you and is easy for you to remember as this will make it easier to find papers when you are looking for them again. For example, some might use the words *Auto Insurance* and others *Car Insurance* when labeling.

Whenever possible discard obsolete catalogs, outdated coupons, and unneeded paperwork. If you don't absolutely need it, throw it away or shred it. In many cases, you can probably find the information you need online or can retrieve another copy if you need it later. Be ruthless and discard everything but the essentials.

Once you've sorted all the paperwork, label folders to match your index cards and file the paperwork in appropriate manila folders. Organize the manila file folders, one folder each inside a hanging file folder, in your file container in A-Z order for easy retrieval of information at a moment's notice.

Put the file container in a convenient spot for putting away more paperwork as you find it, but remember that a wise home manager doesn't save any more paperwork than is absolutely necessary. Do a little work now to create a system that functions and gain a habit of filing paperwork on a regular basis. A functional filing system makes all the difference in controlling household papers.

14

Your Password Cracker

Keeping track of regularly used electronic usernames and passwords is confusing. Most people have a piece of information here, another bit there, and sometimes nowhere at all (except in their busy heads). You might not want to use your computer to remember some of your usernames and passwords for security reasons. Maybe you're also worried about writing things down and someone else finding them.

To partially solve this challenge, you might consider setting up a useable system to keep the non-security information on a specific hard copy. On page 40 is an *Internet Username and Password* form to show you how to get your frequently used Internet usernames and passwords formally organized. It is also available free at *www.houseoforder.com/downloads.htm.*

Although you may feel like having a central log of usernames and passwords is risky, it will get rid of all those scraps of paper floating around on your desk and save you time when you don't have to hunt for the right post-it note. As you record the information on this form, discard your scraps and notes. Eliminate the mess while you still preserve the information. If you're not worried about forgetting the password, use asterisks for some of the characters or numbers of the password on the form. This will give you a clue as to the whole password while increasing security.

Make sure that you use different passwords to meet different needs, rather than always using the same one. This is more secure, especially for more sensitive information.

If you keep this information on the username and password form in a secret place, your electronic interactions will be much easier. You'll be able to easily access Internet sites that are important to you no matter how infrequently you might return to them because the entrance information has been written down in one place.

Please be careful and keep this information safely and securely stored, even as it kept convenient enough for occasional reference needs. By using this tool and these methods, your life will improve dramatically on and off the Internet.

Name_____

	Internet site	User name	Email address	Password	Date
1					
2					
3					
4					
5					
6					
7					
8					
9					
10					
11					
12					
13					
14					
15					
16					
17					
18					
19					
20					

15

Take Control of Endless Emails

I love email. I use it as often as the phone and appreciate its convenience. But even with its usefulness, a lot of us struggle with email organization. Here's one inquiry:

Marie, do you have email organization tips? No matter what, I am always behind on emails. I am behind on replying to friends, I am behind on reading information I have requested, and I am behind in responding to family.

I try not to reply to my personal emails too soon or others will just keep emailing me daily. Then I will need to respond again. Do you see the endless cycle? Being behind is stressful, to say the least. I don't want to offend others, but I just get so behind! What are some possible answers? Candice

I have found several good techniques for keeping up and yet being in charge of my email correspondence.

After I read an email, I write a response right away. This means I don't have to take the time to reread email at a later time. If I don't want to send this response too soon, however, I save it as a draft. Part of my Monday morning routine is to send off my email drafts. This keeps me sane and tells my friends that most responses from me will take up to a week.

Sometimes I get a second response right away (and often within the hour). Again, I write my response right away, save it, and then send it out the following Monday. This has slowed down my immediate responders turn around time and given me more time to focus on other priorities.

Try to keep your own emails short and to the point. This will set an example for people who write you of what you expect.

For example, if I need an important question answered, I use an asterisk at the beginning of the sentence and put the sentence at the beginning of a separate paragraph. This emphasizes the information I need without having to repeat myself in a second email.

For example:

> * Will you be bringing the portable crib when you come to visit?
>
> * Can you send along your address and phone number so I can mail the package to you?
>
> * Do you want me to bring three or four dozen cupcakes for the party?

If I'm not ready to reply to an email, I move it to a folder marked *Answer Sometime*. This helps me take control of my time. For me, sometimes these emails wait for days, sometimes more than a month. Having them in a special folder keeps them convenient without keeping them in my face.

I usually look at *Answer Someday* emails on the first Monday of every month. Sometimes I write responses, other times I leave the email in the *Answer Someday* folder for a later, better time for reply. Occasionally, I will discard the email as I have lost interest or have talked to the person face to face.

With good email organization, you can correspond electronically with others and still maintain a sense of sanity. Emails are not meant to be a pressure in your life; they are meant to have purpose and be a pleasure.

16

Organize Digital Photos

Your digital photos need to be organized in a way so they are easy to file and even easier to retrieve.

Any time you attempt to get organized on the computer, think in three directions:

1) Do I have the tools to get organized?

2) Do I have a logical, reliable system?

3) Do I have a routine that functions and works with the tools and the system I have set up?

First, create a holding folder where photographs can be kept until they are processed. On my computer, I call this folder *Photos to Process.*

Anytime you download or upload pictures, create a new subfolder in *Photos to Process.* Title the subfolder with information about the people, date, place, and/or occasion of the photos. For example, I might title a subfolder as follows: *2009-03~Ricks, Brian, Birthday, Highland, Utah*. By putting the year first and then the month, I'm automatically ordering the *Photos to Process* subfolders chronologically.

Create another main folder where you will keep photos permanently. I label this folder *Processed Photos*, and within this folder I keep subfolders labeled with names, topics, and events.

Because most of my photos are historical, I like organizing my subfolders by family members' names. I have one main subfolder that says *Photos~Ricks' Family*. Within that subfolder there are additional subfolders entitled *Photos~Ricks, James*, which are the photographs for my immediate family, and *Photos~Ricks, Norman* which are photographs for my father-in-law's family. By first listing the surname and then given name, I can find and file my pictures easily.

Within the *Photos~Ricks, James* subfolder, I have additional sub-subfolders labeled:

> *Photos~Ricks, James~2007*
>
> *Photos~Ricks, James~2008*
>
> *Photos~Ricks, James~2009*

Within the *Photos~Ricks, James~2007* subfolder I have that year's event subfolders, such as:

> *2007-08~Ricks, James, UGA Graduation, Athens, Georgia*
>
> *2007-10~Ricks, James, Birthday, Highland, Utah*

I always including the date (with year first), name, event, and place as part of that folder's name.

Here are more examples of my photo organization hierarchy:

📁 **Photos to Process**

    📁 *2009~Ricks, James, Easter, Highland, Utah*

    📁 *2009~Ricks, James, Father's Day, SLC, Utah*

📁 **Processed Photos**

    📁 *Photos~Ricks' Family*

      📁 *Photos~Ricks, James*

        📁 *Photos~Ricks, James~2007*

          📁 *2007-08~ jnr, UGA Graduation, Athens, Georgia*

          📁 *2007-10~jnr, Birthday, Highland, Utah*

        📁 *Photos~Ricks, James~2008*

          📁 *2008-06~jnr, SLC, Utah*

        📁 *Photos~Ricks, James~2009*

          📁 *2009-01~tmr, Birthday, Highland, Utah*

As I process my photos, I label each file with the initials of those people in the photograph, the date of the photograph, and the place of the photograph. For instance: *2007-08, jnr, UGA Graduation, Athens, Georgia.* Using people's initials helps me keep an abbreviated record of everyone that is in the photograph. If there is a special event of which I have taken several photographs of the same people, I will add to those photograph file titles numbers such as 1, 2, 3, 4, and 5 as needed. For example:

2007-08, jnr, UGA Graduation, Athens, Georgia~01

2007-08, jnr, UGA Graduation, Athens, Georgia~02

2007-08, jnr, UGA Graduation, Athens, Georgia~03

In order to organize your digital photos, you need to setup the necessary folders on your computer, set up a system for labeling and organizing the computer photo files and folders, and keep a good routine. I generally organize my *Photos to Process* weekly. Keeping up with your photo filing will make finding photographs so much easier.

Take the time to organize your own digital photos. Think of tools, a system, and a routine that will function for you.

ORGANIZATION CHALLENGES

17

Organization Monsters

Where I live, it often snows heavily in the winter. Sometimes the storms are silent nighttime monsters that leave some eight inches of snow on the ground and are quietly gone before light. When we go outside to a good three hours of shoveling work, my family doesn't know quite where to begin.

Isn't that how it is with all big challenges, especially the big organization monsters? Where do you begin, how do you proceed? What kind of time and stamina will it take to finish— and where did the monster come from anyway?

When we began shoveling snow after the last monster snow storm, we decided to start at the corner of the garage and make snow-shovel wide pathways to the front door, down the driveway, around to the garage can, and over to the mailbox. Then if our energy or time gave out, we could at least function.

After we had the narrow walking pathways dug out, we decided to clear part of the driveway so we could get the vehicles to the street for errands, meetings, and work. This focused our energies on clearing a vehicle-wide pathway so family members could drive away to their appointments in a timely manner.

Taking breaks was very important. After a good amount of work, we stopped and admired our progress and planned the next projects: clearing the front sidewalk and porch, making a wider path from the garbage can to the street, and clearing the street sidewalks.

Our muscles were sore and the problem still seemed overwhelming, but we knew we had to keep at it. Sometimes putting your head down without worrying about finishing and just going to work really helps the project move along.

We took a second break when our stomachs began to rumble, got some breakfast, and then returned with renewed energy and a happier attitude because the necessities—the paths to the mailbox, car, and garage—were already done.

Tackle your organization monsters the best way that you can. Make up a short plan, take a break, return with a medium plan, take another break, continue with a long plan, and keep at it until the end.

18

From Frazzled and Frustrated to Focused

We all have days when we feel frazzled and frustrated. These difficult days make our lives feel unfocused and unappealing. To go from frazzled and frustrated to focused, 1) cut down your commitments by ten percent, 2) look good to feel good, and 3) simplify the dirty jobs.

Usually, you feel frazzled because you are trying to do too much in too little time. Try cutting down the demands on you by ten percent. This will give you room to take care of your most important responsibilities first with your best energy.

Think about your daily routines and where you can make some changes and remove extra tension. Do you need to have your daughter wait in the foyer of the music store so you won't have to go looking for her and thus can save time when picking her up from piano lessons? Do you need to cook twice as much half as often and serve leftovers every other evening to reduce time as the family's cook? Do you need to spend an hour this Saturday updating your wardrobe so you can be ready for next week's business trip?

Even if you feel frazzled, you don't have to look it (and looking good will help you feel better). Always dress one level higher than your mood so you feel attractive even when you are doing laundry, dishes, or taking care of the children. Put on some earrings or lipstick, do your hair, and wear a cute outfit. Dressing up will lift your mood and focus your energies on positive action. Others will also respect you more when you are dressed nicer.

Sometimes you get frazzled and frustrated because the chores and responsibilities you hate keep making demands on you. Everyone has household jobs they do not like. It might be dusting, vacuuming, laundry, bills, dishes, or something else. It might even be all of these things!

Focus on one of these challenges each week until you have closely scrutinized and resolved them. Examine the responsibility and decide how you can move from frustrated to focused. How can you make this job take less of your time (and therefore generate less frustration)? Try rearranging the order in which you clean that room, the way you fold the towels, or how many socks you keep in that drawer.

Focus on improving and implementing new ideas to minimize your frustration and maximize your effort and focus. Buy better containers for sorting laundry. Paint the kitchen a color that you like. Reorganize so emptying the dishwasher will be faster and easier.

Look at the demands in your life—from home, family, work, and others. Take a look at what makes you feel frustrated and frazzled. Ask yourself what you can do to decrease your commitments, dress a little nicer, and organize a bit more so you can increase the control and focus in your life.

You will feel better, you will see things more clearly, and you will endure the bad days better.

19

Think It Through

When life is complex, you can't afford to make major mistakes, leave things behind, or retrace your steps and deal with the challenges and substantial delays that go with mishaps.

At one time in my life I had several major events happening all in one summer: a son returning from a foreign country, another son getting married, a third son moving across country, and a fourth son starting a new job. I had to plan for all of these events at once. This concentrated summer needed special planning and preparation. I had to think things through carefully.

The same sort of complexity in your life could be a day trip to another city, giving a professional presentation, or preparing for a vacation. In all complex situations—small or big—always remember to think it through.

As you think it through, take some time alone to formulate a written plan. Thinking it through on paper will help you not to worry, which will help you sleep better and function at a higher level. Think through an upcoming event and answer these questions: "Have I remembered everything? Will I have on hand what I need when I need it? How will I dress to accommodate the volatile weather? What will I do when I'm asked that embarrassing question?"

When you move from worrying to thinking it through, you might consider role-playing. If you are taking a trip, for instance, role-play getting up on a specific, upcoming morning and dress yourself, thus confirming what clothes you need to pack. Think through what tools and materials you might need for the evening speaking commitment and what items need to be put in the car. Think through the sequence of the important day and see where you need more planning and preparation.

Whether it is an upcoming wedding, a major surgery, or changing jobs, carefully thinking it through will save lots of time and trouble and prevent disasters. Think it through, write down your plans, make sure you are prepared, and then proceed with greater confidence.

20

Deal with Double Discouragements

I have had a good friend who struggled with the repetitive discouragement of being morning sick while parenting a difficult child. When she was newly pregnant the second time, she wasn't sure how she could go through with the process again. She was both discouraged about being a good mother to her first child and feeling ill most of every day. She had what I call double discouragements.

While your double discouragements might be because of difficulties at home or challenges at work, they need not paralyze you. You can move forward with reflection and positive action.

Counter the double (or sometimes tripe and quadruple) discouragements with some resolution and courage. No matter how bad today is, tomorrow might be better or it might be worse. If it is likely to get better, you can smile some more. If it is going to be worse, it will be tough going. However tomorrow will turn out, today it is time to get out a piece of paper and begin a written list to focus on what you can do with your situation instead of focusing on what is discouraging you. This list will have three column headings:

1) What is on my mind?

2) What can I do about what's on my mind?

3) Where do I start to move from these challenges to possible solutions?

After acknowledging your dilemmas and making a list of your troubles, take a few minutes to focus on something you can do from your newly made list.

For example, my friend decided to teach her daughter how to spell her first and last name to feel some parenting progress. She also determined to ask her spouse to take care of their child when he got home from work for a half hour so she could have a parenting break while she cooked a nice evening meal for the family. Just knowing the break was coming and that dinner preparations could be somewhat delayed improved things considerably during the period of her morning sickness.

Doing something, anything, will make your challenges fade momentarily and make a bad day just a bit brighter. At work or home, diverting momentarily to a small project on your list will help calm and settle you. Some progress is better than just feeling miserable. Just a few minutes of focusing on developing solutions can help you see the day through. Write down your goals, figure out a small, short beginning project, and go to work.

21

Change the Unchangeable

Change is hard. It is hard for each of us personally and even harder to persuade others to change with you. The following email is an example of a problem with change:

Hi Marie — How can those of us who are set in our ways evolve and change for the better?

My specific example would be my kitchen trash can. I really should have, and I have room to have, three recycle bins instead of one large kitchen waste can. Why is it so hard to change to three smaller bins (one for soda cans, one for plastics, and one for trash)?

How can I change and how can I get my family on board? How do I make change work? Thanks! Lisa

When desiring permanent change, understanding and applying three principles always seems to help.

First, change happens best when you set up an environment that makes change convenient. In the case of the trash bins, this means purchasing three smaller bins (each a different color) and placing them in the kitchen. Change can only happen once these supplies are set up.

The second step is to practice the new behavior in a setting where family members can learn the proper procedures and rules without embarrassment or time pressure. Have a practice session (maybe even make it a family game) and do the new behavior over and over again. Mix empty milk cartons, cereal boxes, and soda cans in a large container and hold a contest to see who can get the items properly sorted fastest.

Third, desired changes will become more habitual if you frequently review how the new habit is working (after one week, two weeks, three weeks, and then a month) and decide what fine-tuning needs to happen, like more clear distinction between bins or adding a requirement that cans are crushed before they're thrown in the bin.

Look for one place in your life where you are struggling with change and apply these principles:

1) Set up the appropriate environment,

2) Practice at the new habit, and

3) Review routines and reset procedures as needed.

Diagnose what your problems are, make plans, and work towards new habits. Then change is certain.

22

Withdraw, Regroup, and Reemerge

During challenging weeks, when you get stressed and you can't handle life, keep these principles in mind: withdraw, regroup, and reemerge.

When stress is heavy, the first step to bringing order back to is to withdraw, to retract a pace or two. Head towards your master bedroom if you are at home, go to the restroom if you are at work, or take a walk.

After you have withdrawn, it is time to regroup. Take a moment and review your priorities. Decide if it is going to be cornflakes again for dinner, if your spouse can handle the laundry tonight, or if your teenager can manage your two other children so you can have an hour alone in the home office to work uninterrupted. For a few moments, take time to regroup and review how you can handle pressures differently and better.

After you have withdrawn and regrouped, it is time to re-emerge again. When you do, take a moment to notify those around you that things will need to be a little different.

"No, I am not going to go to that meeting tonight."

"Yes, I am planning on a simple dinner."

"No, I won't be able to wash those pants until Saturday."

"Yes, I would appreciate some babysitting help this evening."

It is up to you to make life work for your family, in your workplace, and all through your life. When life is challenging and stressful, it is also up to you to withdraw a pace, regroup to find better organization possibilities, and then reemerge with a sense of control.

When you take time to withdraw, regroup, and reemerge, those around you will appreciate your being back on top of life again and you will get more done and be happier.

23

Time to Catch Up

We all get behind sometimes. It can happen so quickly. All at once you wake up one morning with mountains of laundry stacked all over the house, a pile of letters and bills to reply to, and a dozen other items that need your attention. It is so disheartening!

Some of us face being behind once in a while and a few of us live with it all the time. It is so hard to always be in catch-up mode.

As soon as you realize you're behind, start to take steps to gain control again. A good place to start is to get your visual world in order: put the wash away, get a load of dishes going, sweep the kitchen floor, and straighten the piles of paperwork.

After your visual environment is in order, start to tackle specific projects, like paperwork. Pay the bills, file that stack of receipts, recycle the rack of old newspapers, and write that letter.

Keep up a good pace and focus until you are in control again. While you're in catch-up mode, it is best not to answer the phone, look at your emails, turn on the TV, or respond to your front door bell. Minimizing these and other distractions will help focus your energy. A lot of things can wait until you have gained a sense of renewed organization.

After getting your visual surroundings neat and your high priority projects under control, sit down with your planner and formulate a plan of how you will get caught up with everything else and stay on top of things. List your to-dos one by one. Then prioritize them. Decide what "A" items to do on what days, what "B" items to leave until a little later, and what "C" items can be put aside for much later.

Once you get back into control and on top of things, take some time to brainstorm how you can prevent getting so behind again in the future. Schedule longer *launching* and *landing* time periods—time to gear up and prepare for an event and then more time to settle down afterward—for major projects, events, and activities. · Leaving extra time to gear up for and settle down from big events will keep you from getting behind in your normal routines when foreseeable challenges and big projects come your way.

While you may only need a twenty-minute bubble before and after the normal comings and goings in life, plan at least a one-day launch and land bubble before and after more significant events such as weddings, funerals, graduations, celebrations, and holidays. More significant life events like moving, having a baby, recovering from major surgery, or changing jobs may even require a one-week or even longer launch and land bubble to sufficiently allow for catching back up.

Remember, others will likely push you to the very limit of what you will allow. If you allow less interruptions until you have caught up, you will still be respected and will better be able to respond to life's many demands. May you find your "I can do this and this and no more, no sooner than this" balance, especially as you catch your breath and get caught up again.

24

Confront Personal Confusion

Becoming confused can be very frustrating. It often happens when too many requirements are made of your time, energy, and resources in too short of a time. A long day with sick children, an unexpected death in the family, and even a crazy day fulfilling others' needs can cause this temporary inadequacy. Sometimes you may simply feel confused, others times you feel confusion to the point of intimidation, and more often than not you can be completely overcome by the confusion and thus become somewhat dysfunctional.

When this happens in your life, how can you get a grip? Where do you start to gain control again? What you do to regain a semblance of order? Step by step, you can take control and better handle feeling slightly confused, feeling intimidated, and conquer being completely overcome by confusion.

I would like to suggest when you feel even just slightly confused, instead of continuing on with whatever you're doing, stop and ponder. Sometimes by just stopping and figuring out what's going on, you gain understanding and perspective. For example, you may be a little bit confused because the laundry is overly large today and you've got stains on three of your boys' shirts that look difficult to get out. Or, maybe you are confused because you haven't decided what you want to serve for dinner tonight and thus haven't gotten any meat out of the freezer. Start figuring out what you need to do now to reduce and eliminate your confusion. Then you can return to your work with greater confidence.

If you are feeling intimidated by confusion, you have moved to being somewhat overwhelmed by the confusion that surrounds you. When you do feel this intimidation, you should stop and ponder as before, but also go one more step and formulate a more formal plan of action.

For instance, maybe you are feeling confused because three different friends have suggested three different options for the next scrapbooking project you are planning. So when you feel confused, stop and ponder.

"Okay, I'm confused. I'm feeling put upon and intimidated. Exactly what will I do to get back to a place that's more peaceful, where I feel more in control? I'll plan on using Mary's idea this month and invite her to have the gathering at her home. I'll ask Nancy and Beth to bring refreshments. I'll buy the scrapbooking supplies."

When you again feel enlightened, a simple written list of activities and projects will bring you back on task.

Lastly, there are times in your life when you are completely overcome by confusion to the point of becoming dysfunctional. It might be because you have been under the weather for three days. Or, it might be because you have unexpected visitors overstaying their welcome. Or, it might be because you woke up this morning with the flu and haven't done much more than eat and sleep all day long. When you do feel overcome by confusion, it is probably because it's going to be a few days or maybe even a week or so before you will be back in control. Even in your current distress, you can feel the future stress!

In this case, you not only need to stop, ponder, and create a written plan of action for *now*, but you need an additional written list of what you will do to come back to order *when* your energy returns, the illness abates, or you're unexpected company disappears. You can't do much now but make a written list of what your future plans will be, but these notations will move the worry from your head to paper and let your soul rest.

As you face confusion, follow these steps to stop feeling confused, to stop being intimidated by confusion, and to stop becoming completely dysfunctional. Simply stop, ponder, create a written plan of immediate action, and another written list of future steps to bring things back to order!

25

Bad News
to Good Progress

The news has been pretty bad lately. Fuel prices are fluctuating, housing prices are volatile, food is getting more expensive, and job opportunities are nebulous. This up/down news can be somewhat upsetting and leave you feeling downtrodden! It also causes you to worry and feel a certain sense of panic. It can lead to spinning your wheels and consequently making little progress towards your current goals.

However, organization demands a different approach. You see, moving from bad news to good progress means addressing right away four possible items of major importance:

When you are particularly stressed, four projects seem to settle things down in your mind and heart:

1) Get more food stocked away in your pantry or storage room (the sooner the better).

2) Figure out how to earn more and/or spend less so the family budget has greater flexibility (creativity enters in here).

3) Decide how to reduce vehicle use or multiply the errands completed each time you are out and about.

4) Calculate how to potentially secure the financial future of your family with more education or training to increase your career options.

Moving from bad news to good progress *also* means asking four questions:

1) Where are you lacking the most in bringing security to your current situation?

2) What can reasonably be done now to improve your circumstances?

3) Who in your family can do what to solve these challenges?

4) When will you begin to act upon your decisions?

Moving from bad news to good progress in an organized manner means taking your goals and choosing small, simple, and reasonably short tasks and begin accomplishing them. (Remember, every marathon happens one step at a time.)

For instance, you might pick up two cases of canned fruit at the store during your next grocery-shopping trip to fill out your pantry storage. You might try making homemade cookies next weekend to spend less money on groceries and thus have more funds for the family budget. You could walk to a nearby neighbor's instead of jumping into the car for that upcoming birthday party. You might even polish up on some older, but useful skills to renew your creative moneymaking powers.

Can you see that it isn't complex? It isn't always the big things! It isn't just major changes! It is a little reduction here, a small change there, a simple shift here, and a focused effort there. Receiving bad news will happen from time to time, but you don't need to succumb to it. Instead, make some good progress after considering the problems, resolving upon solutions, and beginning specific projects to find partial answers right away. This will always help you maintain a more orderly life.

26

Transition Times

From time you will go through periods of transition. Things change in your exterior world and also inside your heart. It is confusing and definitely challenging as change inevitably pulls you along. For example, there might be an addition to your family, the death of a friend, sudden job changes, an unexpected move, prolonged illness, and/or an occasional natural catastrophe to take their toll on your soul.

When you are going through this kind of transition, there are several principles that can help you thrive in the midst of change.

It is essential to cling to daily routines. Prayer, scripture or other good book reading, journaling, exercise, and making yourself attractive every day provide a firm foundation to your present fragility and provide an outward confidence to belie your inward turmoil. Keep up on your personal needs  and dress up past your mood to maintain and sustain your capacity to cope.

It is also vital to focus on today's needs. You may have little capacity to think out a week, a month, or into the year ahead. But you can handle today. For example, you might clean out a clogged downspout, take a small gift to the friend having outpatient surgery tomorrow, pick up last weekend's messes in the living room, and file some of your paperwork. You can function in *today*. For now, tomorrow will have to take care of itself.

It is important to have a non-judgmental, understanding friend to confide in, one who won't give you answers, but will listen, love, and hug. Such a friend won't repeat your conversations and is priceless during personal change.

It is imperative to keep going, slogging through the difficult hours, keeping busy during the long evenings, and planning what to do to keep your hands and head active while your heart figures out this new terrain.

Transition periods are significant times of growth, for they prove you can be pliable. Writing down your volatile thoughts, struggling through your emotions, and letting the feelings sit until they are ready to leave is all right. You don't rush your response to change. It comes, you embrace it, let it hurt or heal, and you go on.

Transition may be a part of your life right now or it may come soon enough. Look forward, hold steady with daily habits, keep your body moving, and soon the foundation of your soul will settle again into capacity and growth. It has always been so with those I have admired. It will be so again!

27

Stop Before You're Tired

I would like to share some insights about fatigue, weariness, and the general tiredness I see day after day, week after week as I work with men and women striving for order in their lives.

I rarely meet people who are truly lazy. When you're sprawled on the couch and can't even imagine doing one more thing, most of the time you've just pushed yourself way past reasonable limits. Although you might think you have to push this hard in order to get things done or that pushing just a little  harder will help solve a problem, in the long run pushing past your own limits takes more time than stopping before you're tired.

You might respond to this weariness by becoming cranky. Sometimes you oversleep the next day or sometimes if the demands of life make it impossible for you to stop as you would like and rest a bit, you really have repetitively long and difficult days.

When you push yourself to stay up too late, work on a project for too long, and keep up a hectic pace day after day, no matter how much you hope it will not affect your general well-being and your emotional health, it will all catch up to you sometime. All it takes is imagining yourself sprawled out on the couch, dead tired, to realize that weariness is a great enemy to having an orderly life.

If you struggle with pushing too hard, consider these reality checks. First, it's very rare for other people to give you a rest period. It is up to you give yourself the rests you need. Take a moment to sit down and play with the baby. Take five minutes to sit on the back steps and drink a glass of cold water. Take a brisk walk around your work building between meetings. Take a half-hour while the baby is sleeping and read a favorite book.

Second, notice when you get tired during the day. Maybe you have a ten or eleven o'clock in the morning slump. Maybe your energy just drops off right around 4:00 p.m. Recognize these times and stop momentarily before you're too tired. Take a short breather. Do your work standing up instead of sitting down for a few minutes. Turn to a more exciting project instead of continuing a boring one. Leave a challenge alone for a while and instead do a more routine chore so you don't have to think as much for a few minutes.

Third, give yourself extra attention during your slump times to keep your overall strength and energy up throughout the remainder of the day. Remember that it is up to you to go a little slower, stop altogether for a few minutes, or even take a quick nap so you can make it through the day. It is up to you to call your own rest periods.

You might be surprised because even a five-minute change of routine or a momentary switch of focus will make a tremen-dous difference. Take just a few minutes to get some fresh air on the back doorstep. Read just a short chapter in your favorite book. Slow down and nap for a few minutes. All of these diversions can help you get past your weariness so you can continue with normal life.

Look at your daily slump times to see what you can do to take control of your tiredness. Remember to rest before you are too tired to go on. Take care of yourself so you will have the energy to finish out the day with a smile.

ORGANIZATION FOR PARENTS AND CHILDREN

28

Do the Worst Jobs First

Should parents make children do chores before they play? By requiring chores first, parents teach their children the value of prioritizing projects and the satisfaction play brings because the work was done first.

Doing the worst first facilitates strong character and joy in accomplishment. Here are some examples of ways you might encourage those you nurture to do work before play.

"Yes, Marsha, you may play with your dolls after you feed the dog, eat lunch, and tidy up the family room."

"Yes, Joe, you may watch TV later, but let's start the afternoon by reviewing your times tables, weeding your portion of the yard, and putting away your laundry."

Doing the worst applies to you, too. For example, dust first if you don't like it. Then all the rest of today's housework will be easier because the worst is over.

If you have several loads of laundry to fold and really don't enjoy folding socks, do that load first and get it over with.

If you need to clean up the kitchen and hate sweeping under the table, sweep there first.

We all have especially tedious tasks around major holidays. At Thanksgiving, for instance, it might be making or buying pies. Next time, get the pies made, frozen, and off your list by the second week of the month. Then all the other joys of Thanksgiving including family, food, and fun will be more enjoyable.

Think about your Christmas worst first project. It might be finding your greeting card stash and writing your annual family letter. Try getting the whole job done and in the mailbox during the first week of the month. You can almost feel your Christmas excitement growing with the thought of the letter and those holiday greetings cards finished and mailed.

Doing the worst first is also useful when dealing with difficult people. If Aunt Mattie is your most troublesome relative and is likely to make a rude comment to you at the upcoming wedding, approach her as soon as she arrives, compliment her outfit, and accept her inevitable criticism with a smile and be done with it. Then the rest of the festivities can be more pleasurable and fun.

Remember, doing the worst first always makes the rest best!

29

The Oops Syndrome

The oops syndrome is any action or situation causing you or others embarrassment. You probably tend to have the same embarrassing experiences over and over again. Maybe you leave the zipper undone on your skirt, are partial to losing keys (if only momentarily), and have missed more than one meeting simply because while you were told about it, you didn't take the time to write down the details in your planner or on your calendar.

Sometimes, you will also find the oops syndrome prevalent in your family. You might have a child that regularly loses sweaters, another that does very poorly on his spelling tests, or a third child that consistently misses her piano practicing and has a dozen excuses for why she has failed you, again. And, of course, there are also oops syndrome challenges to which you adjust in your personal life because it is unlikely your spouse will change much.

It is time to take care of the oops problems in your life. Let's start with you first. Every time you find this kind of disorganization entering your life, stop and look for ways to live around the challenge, to change your situation so that the oops syndrome does not continue.

For example, you may play the organ at your church. This means you probably have keys to open the church house and the organ so that when you arrive you can practice and then take care of your responsibilities. However, when you put the keys in your bag that also contains your hymnbook, the keys instantly sink to the bottom of the bag and are always hard to find at the door. And, more than once, you may have gone all the way to the church only to find that the keys are not in the bottom of the bag at all.

In an attempt to solve this problem, you might look for a bag with a clasp where you can click your keys right at the top of the bag and know instantly rather or not the organ keys are in the right place.

This is the first step to removing the oops syndrome: gain the right tools in order to reverse the effects or completely elimi-nate oops from in your life.

The second step is to create a system. In the case of the organ keys, you would need to establish a habit of putting your organ keys back on the clip at the top of your bag every time you play the organ, which means both when you practice on Sunday morning and again after you actually play during the meeting.

After you have attempted to conquer one of your own oops challenges, you might take the opportunity to do the same thing with your family members, one by one. How is the best way to keep sweaters from being lost? How can you improve the poor spelling test results? What is to be done about those missed piano practices?

Think about the oops syndromes in the situations in your life and consider ways to resolve them one at a time. Work with others who are failing or being humiliated because of their oops embarrassments. The challenge is to replace the previous oops behavior with new habits.

It is possible that some people you love, who are constantly causing you oops syndrome disappointment, are not likely to change much. Figure out ways to live around this fact. Maybe you can keep spare cash in your wallet to save embarrassment when your spouse has empty pockets and there is need for parking meter change. Try asking for help earlier than usual to give your loved one enough time to function responsibly or ask for more than is needed so that what is given will be sufficient.

Remember, the oops syndrome doesn't need to be a part of your life ever again. There are ways to solve this syndrome by gaining tools, increasing talents, and establishing good habits. And when nothing is likely to change in another person's habits, figure out ways to work around the oops personality all together.

30

Teach Others to Wait

A delicate but very important skill for anyone trying to bring more order to his or her life is the skill of teaching others to wait. One of the great challenges in life is knowing when to stop your own tasks, how fast to respond to another's needs, and what to do when others call for you, the phone rings, or children require your attention.

You will bring greater order into your life by not trying to be everything to everyone all the time. For example, you are folding laundry and your child says,

"Mom, I need you to come and ...."

Generally, you might drop what you are doing and run to the child's aid. If the child is capable of understanding the concept of waiting, you might do better to say,

"Johnny, I would be happy to come and help you. However, I have about three more minutes of folding towels, two more minutes of putting them away, and then I'll be there."

This method of teaching others to wait allows you to come to finishing points, mini-finishing points though they may be, so you have places of finishing in your routines.

So, the concept simply is: As you go through life and your children mature, or your teenagers and spouse are cooperative, or your coworkers and elderly parents are understanding, let them know you are happy to come, but you would appreciate it if they would wait (if only for a bit) so you can come to a finishing point.

"Yes, Mom, I can hear you calling and I know you would like me to come and chat at your bedside. I'll be there momentarily. I just need to put the spaghetti sauce in the casserole dish and turn on the oven."

Or, when you answer the phone and a request is made to run an errand, say,

"You know honey, I would be happy to do that for you right away. However, I am in the middle of scrubbing the kitchen floor. It will take me about 20 minutes to finish and then I'll be happy to leave and run the errand. Will that work?"

If you begin to employ this tactic, when circumstances are such that you do have the opportunity, you bring your life to places of finishing. The laundry gets folded and also put away, the kitchen floor gets scrubbed and the chairs put back around the table, and dinner is prepared in a timely manner. You will feel more in control.

At the same time, you are also instilling a sense of self-respect in yourself and teaching others to respect you. Observe carefully your interactions and see where you are jumping to someone's aid too quickly; and therefore, leaving your current task undone in favor of helping someone else right away. Let others wait, if even just momentarily, so you can come to a wonderful, complete, and sensible finishing point. Consistently teach others to wait to increase order in your life.

31

Summer Chores
for Children

If you are on a traditional school schedule, when it starts
getting warmer and school will soon be out, it is time to make
some summer plans about what your children (no matter their
ages) will be expected to do this summer in addition to outings,
vacations, and other activities. It is best to focus in three areas:

1) What will be the daily neatness standards for their
   bedrooms during the upcoming summer? Beds made?
   Clothes picked up? Curtains open, drawers closed, and
   toys picked up? Will these responsibilities need to be
   done before breakfast, before daily chores, or before
   they are allowed to play with friends?

2) What household
   skills will you teach
   them during this va-
   cation time? Will
   they be in charge of
   making one *general
   use* room neat each
   morning? Will they
   dust, vacuum, and

clean another room once a week? Will they have chores in your yard and maybe a garden portion to weed, water, and harvest? Will they learn to cook (maybe at lunchtime)?

3) What reading opportunities will you offer? When will you be going to the library week to week? Where will the library books be kept? During what hour of the day will you arrange for quiet time so family members can read or do other quiet projects without interruption, distraction, or other disturbances?

As the days grow hot, it is time to take just a moment to think through your upcoming summer plans:

1) Daily neatness standards for bedrooms you will uphold,

2) Household chores and cooking skills you will share, and,

3) Reading opportunities you will offer.

During the weeks preceding summertime; set up a simple and effective chore schedule for your children. Your chore plan for each child should include a little vacuuming, a little dusting, and some cleaning of bathrooms. Weeding a bit would be nice, and taking care of a vehicle also beneficial.

Remember, parenthood is not a popularity contest. You are in charge to make the rules, provide the opportunities to work and learn, and protect the time for personal reading.

May the upcoming summer and every summer be different because you take a few minutes to formulate and implement your plans, decide what skills to teach, and create a daily break for personal reading.

As a side note, when your family is on a year-round school schedule, these same skills could be taught during off-school weeks. It will be more difficult to establish a routine cadence because the vacation times will be shorter, but it is very important for children to be regularly responsible for part of the household maintenance.

32

Tell, Teach, Time, and Self-Initiative

Just as non-school time offers a great situation to focus on helping your children learn to enjoy their specific chores, it also offers a great time to teach a healthy work ethic and a positive attitude. There is usually more time for instruction, more leisure for checking to make sure jobs are done correctly, and more capacity for patience without a lot of outside pressures. There are four important concepts to consider as you approach teaching proper work habits and attitudes.

1) Specifically tell them what their jobs will entail so there is no misunderstanding as to the desired end results. This will help them understand that standards have been set and they are to be met.

2) Teach them how to appropriately do their jobs. This will demonstrate the methods and skills required for success.

3) Time how long it takes them to complete each job for several days. This helps introduce the concept that if you do a job repetitively and are diligent, you can do it better and you can do it faster.

4) Finally, teach them the concept of self-initiative, one of the most important principles a young child, teenager, or even an adult can learn. There can be great self-satisfaction in doing your jobs without being asked.

Anyone that lives in a home should participate in maintaining it. Tell your children that house and yard work are part of this upcoming summer's activities. With the introduction of simple but repetitive jobs, include the standards desired, teach the methods required, show them that practice makes it faster, and help them move to self-initiative. With their help, they can do much to make the load lighter for maintaining the home, cleaning the yard, and keeping up with the laundry.

Take plenty of time, at the beginning, to teach them the right way to do each job. If this teaching is not done appropriately, there will be frustration, sullenness, and disappointment all through the long summer months. Work with the children and a timer as they do each job to show them how long it takes to do it properly. Then repeat the timed sequence as they do the job again and again to show they can get better each and every time they do their chores with focus and diligence.

Over and over speak of self-initiative. Reward them generously for any self-initiative that is shown in an appropriate way. For instance, have special colored drinking glasses at dinner for those members of your family who do their chores during the day without being asked. In other words, when they show self-initiative, let everyone know about it. It becomes a symbol of their achievements and their willingness to cooperate.

Again, after deciding who will do what and how much each person will be responsible for, take time to describe the job completely. Teach them how to do the work sufficient to your set standards. Then, time your children so they get better and better at their jobs in less and less time, and finally introduce the concept of self-initiative with all its long-term advantages.

May the forthcoming summertime be more fulfilling as you and your whole family work together towards a more orderly life!

33

Warm Weather Clothing Standards

It is useful to order your life with specific warm weather clothing standards for your family. It is not so important what your standards of modesty are as much as it is important that there are limits, barriers, and well-understood boundaries. Parents and guardians who leave those decisions to others' best judgment soon find that others don't have such great judgment. Instead, set standards that everyone can support about what is allowable, what doesn't work, and what will be considered completely inappropriate. This helps family members in three ways.

First, children tend to grow up more morally safe when standards are set, because in their own mind there are barriers of behavior, dress, and language that have been imposed by their parents or guardians. It also helps them to self-impose their own standards when they become independent and live away from home.

While you may also set standards for language and behavior, deciding upon family clothing standards is a first, easy step in solidifying what is acceptable clothing for your family.

Second, children learn there is clothing that is appropriate and other clothing that is inappropriate from your family's point of view. It is important to talk about these things before your daughter or son brings home the first piece of clothing that raises your spouse's eyebrows and causes your own mouth to drop. Be specific about lengths, tightness, looseness, exposure, and extremes.

Third, your children will likely push against these family standards more than once and it is important there are carefully clarified parental parameters. Because you will be buying some of these clothes, remember that something returned to the store shelf is harder to wear than something purchased and sitting in a chest of drawers. Also, just because it was received as a gift, doesn't necessarily mean that it is acceptable to wear in your home.

If you do not want your girls to have midriff exposure, they should know that before they bring home the first piece of clothing showing that intriguing bit of skin. If you want his pants to be a certain length, that should be discussed before purchases are made. If you want modesty to be practiced between shower and bedroom, discuss methods and appropriate clothing for movement between rooms.

How low will allowable necklines be? Will exposed cleavage be in your best interests? Will see-through or partially see-through fabric be allowed? Will sleeveless tops, two-piece swimsuits, and short shorts be a part of your family's wardrobe? Will off-the-hip pants be endured?

If you are married, discuss what warm weather clothing standards mean to both of you. Then continue the discussion with your whole family until the standards can be set down in writing. These standards can then be posted for all to review and will be helpful when clothing is purchased, borrowed, or worn.

This will order your life and your family's life from the inside out so that each member knows what your clothing standards are in easy-to-state terms. It will help your children feel safe. It will help you be more comfortable around your teenage children as they explore differently clothing styles and it will teach them to respond appropriately both when shopping and when dressing.

It is always easier to set standards before the issue becomes an issue than to wait and have to cajole, persuade, or endure! Family dress standards keep everyone unified and family interactions safer and more secure.

34

Summer Stress
and a September List

Right about the end of summer when the heat makes you miserable and your family is driving you slightly strange, it is time to begin a *September List*. This is a list of all those tasks that keep running around in your busy mind that need doing and aren't going to get done any time soon.

You see, summer activities, vacations, visitors, and other pressures move you away from your regular routines. You lose the important, and often very essential, cadence to your lives during the summer months. Thus, the *September List* can alleviate stress, put life into perspective, and allow you to have somewhat of a summer vacation, too.

Begin this written list when your summer days begin to drag, noting those things that will need doing eventually but can wait while you carve watermelon, take the kids to swimming lessons, hike that mountain with your family, and bandage those scrapped knees.

Your mind will relax as you make your list and you can return to making memories because now the *September List* will keep the pressures preserved in writing until everyone is settled down into a routine again with the coming of fall. Then you can tackle that list.

This list making is useful for other seasons as well. Often a *January List* becomes useful right around the middle of November and an *April List* is useful in the middle of February for outdoor projects you would like to address. Whenever you are feeling stressed by and yet unable to tackle the projects troubling your head, begin a new season's list. Happy list making whenever and however it can help relieve that mental strain!

My September List

_____

_____

_____

_____

_____

_____

_____

Until then, it will wait…

35

Regroup When
They Get Grumpy

Grumpy children are really hard to handle and when children's
schedules are modified, their grumpiness seems to magnify
many time over. When sleeping locations are changed, there
are diversions from a regular schedule, and/or there are weekend activities late into the evening, the chance of sibling fights
increases because schedules are shifted and normalcy is
abandoned. It doesn't take much to make the whole family
grumpy.

However, you can work with your children to order their lives
so they (and you) can deal with their grumpiness. There are
three different ways to cure or at least relieve the challenges of
grumpiness in your family.

First, children get grumpy if they don't get enough sleep. This
often means you must alter your schedule accordingly. If they
are going to stay up late the night before, they will need to
either sleep in or take naps the next day. Also, major activities
take a lot of energy, so having them one day after the other,
especially with very young children, can be taxing. A late
activity one night and an early activity the next day just doesn't
work well, either. So, make every effort to help children get

enough sleep each day, either with naps or quiet time after a shortened night's sleep the previous evening.

Second, teach children that weariness is part of life and that it is okay to stop, to curl up, or just lay down for a while even if sleeping isn't likely to happen. Identifying and expressing exhaustion helps everyone to understand what is happening. Of course, you might set the example by indicating to your children at the end of a long morning:

"I'm a bit tired. I'll just sit down for a bit to rest. Maybe after lunch, I'll even take a tiny nap. During that time, the rest of you can nap or read quietly."

Because weariness is inevitable, especially during very stressful or long, drawn out days, help children to understand that is acceptable to be tired and then to rest.

Lastly, help them gain skills to talk through their feelings when they get grumpy. When emotions are running high and weariness/fatigue is added, grumpiness is inevitable.

"George, you seem a bit out of sorts. Tell me how you are feeling inside and then we'll rest a moment on the family room couch."

Talk with your children about why and how grumpiness is manifest in people's lives. Maybe when you're with your children and you observe it another person, you might wish to speak to them about it. When others act ornery, identify the behavior attached to their grumpiness and explain possible reasons for it. This will help them understand grumpiness and how they can perceive it in themselves and other people.

Remember, sometimes it pays to slow down to get more done. Allow your children to get plenty of sleep, help them become aware that they are grumpy, and teach them the skills to communicate about their irritable feelings, and encourage them to take a moment's respite when weariness sets in. Then, your family will be a happier family all around.

36

Teach Children Not to Hit

In many families, hitting is a common way of resolving conflict between siblings. This is not the best way. Is it possible
to teach your family members not to hit? Absolutely! There
are several great skills for ordering your family's emotional life
so conflict is eliminated (or at least reduced) and challenges are
worked through without hitting.

Children that are allowed
to hit as a way of resolving conflicts often become
adults that hit each other
(whether it be as husband
or wife) or parents who
inappropriately hit their
children. This pattern also
leads to inappropriate
moral activities and
variance in social interac-

tions as children mature. When children are allowed to hit
without teaching them how to resolve conflicts appropriately,
trouble is in store.

So begin an initiative in your own home that will change
family interactions for the better. Talk about this new standard
before, after, and during the challenges that are part of living

together. You can begin teaching your children not to hit each other by specifically saying,

"We don't hit in the Smith family."

This will be a little difficult at first because children are very apt at hitting. If they are not taught properly, they are especially good at it when a parent's attention is diverted elsewhere. They get even better at hitting on the sly as they mature. It is time for change now.

When older children squabble with each other and begin hitting, you separate them before resolving the issues and then work with them to verbalize what they are feeling, what happened, and how to find answers. You can teach them to resolve their challenges by talking through their feelings and seeking for a mutual solution. Teach them that mature people do not hit to resolve problems. They talk through their challenges and disputes.

If your children aren't quite ready to have an equitable discussion right after their squabble, separate them until they have cooled down and are a bit more teachable. Then work with them to teach these principles.

Teenagers seem to respond best to a discussion about family interactions and appropriate ways of expressing anger, frustration, and disagreement. Work with them until all parties have a clear perception of what, how, and when disputes will be resolved. Then reinforce these standards both by your own example and by continued training.

Even very small children can be taught. They will often hit or slap you in the face. One of the best ways to work through this is to simply hold their hands softly, but firmly, and say,

"Hitting is not permitted."

They, of course, will do it again just to see what will happen. Again hold their hands and in a soft but firm voice say,

"Hitting is not permitted."

Repeat this over and over again until the child begins to respond and comply.

Lastly, discuss with your spouse better, gentler ways to work through the friction that often happens in a marriage and which might lead, from time to time, to physical hitting. This simply cannot be the best way to have order at home.

So begin a no hitting initiative right away with your family. If you do this, there will be more peace and harmony between your children. There will be more love between you and your spouse as you train by example. There will be more order in your life in general. And, there will be a chance for a new generation to grow up learning how to peacefully handle life's many pressures.

37

The Power of Nurturing

A newly made friend recently told me that when she was a little girl her mother spent hours canning fruit and making jam. They always had homemade bread and her mom sewed beautiful dresses for both her and her older sister. When she was in the seventh grade, her father lost his job, her mother had to go back to work to support the family, and her sister (who was seven years older) went away to college. During the next few years, her mother didn't have time to do those homemaking projects anymore. There was no more canned fruit, bottled jam, or homemade bread.

And so even today, this woman, who is a mother herself, has never done any of these things and does not yet have the skills to do them. It's not so much the exact skills that my friend longs for, it's the feeling of contrast between when she  felt loved, secure, and nurtured and the new feelings of insecurity, loneliness, and sterility. In the end, my friend wishes her mother had somehow, sometime taught her how to sew, can, and cook.

So what homemaking skills do you want to pass on to your sons and daughters? If these skills (and the feelings they engender) are important to you, how can you organize your life to get them passed along? Maybe at holiday time or as a birthday gift, instead of spending quite so much money on things they will simply own, could you give them a certificate *good for* teaching them a skill?

If a holiday is not too far off or birthdays are any time soon, how can you order your life to spend an hour or so to plan and prepare to pass those on these personal legacies?

You see, from my friend's point of view, she would have loved to have had just one afternoon with her mother learning how to bottle jam or bake bread or maybe even just shared an hour with her mom learning the techniques of canning fruit.

It is so important to receive training in certain skills from your parents. I know it is even more important to pass those skills on to the next generation.

So think about it, and in the mix-up and mess of regular routines and challenging times, ask yourself some important questions, consider how to proceed, and then teach. You can truly share this legacy of homemaking skills (whatever they are and however you perceive they will best help your posterity) from generation to generation.

Remember, they will both remember what you taught and more especially that you were the one to teach them.

38

The Answer Is No

When you must say no to others, it is so easy to be weak. You say no, they counter. You begin to explain or discuss or excuse. As soon as you do, you are in a position of weakness and they get the upper hand. Soon the tables are turned and you are moving to:

"Well, maybe...."

"O.K., if you're going to be so hardheaded about it..."

"I don't understand why you won't take no for an answer, but since you won't, then...."

This is not good. If you say no, you have to stick to your no, one hundred percent, super glue stick to it. If you don't mean to say no, then say,

"Maybe..."

"I'll think about it and give in within two minutes..."

"I might as well just say yes and be done with the conflict..."

But you cannot be passive. Submissive parents let their kids get into a little trouble now, which can turn into bigger trouble later. They give in a little bit this time and aren't even asked when the important issues are at stake. Indecisive parents can't easily mentor or have healthy relationships! When you need to say no and do say no, you must to stick to your no.

Somewhere in your relationships there is a person you may frequently give in to even when you don't want or intend to. There is a point where you have to choose between popularity and sound judgment. You probably know who that power person is in your life right now and you know when you regularly recede to, "Well, all right…" after you have rather indecisively said your no.

To bring good order to that relationship and to be taken seriously by all others that surround you, live with you, associate and love you, it is time to take courage. Look in the mirror today and practice,

"I'm sorry. This is *not* up for discussion. I have said no. And no it remains. Whining, pouting, or procrastinating will not change my mind. The answer is NO."

Remember, it is easier to say no sooner than later, firmer than wimpy, and on smaller matters before they become major problems. Go for the no when it is appropriate and stick to it like super glue, because saying no and meaning it will bring much order to your own heart and to the lives of all you influence. Be strong! Someone, meaning you, needs to take a firmer stand! Remember, the answer is NO!

ORGANIZED
FOR BIG EVENTS
AND HOLIDAYS

.

39

Organize for the Holidays

As a holiday happens almost every month of the year in addition to birthdays and other special occasions that need remembering, let's discuss organizing for the holidays. No matter what occasion is coming up, most hosts and hostesses will find that preparing an *Organized for the Holidays* binder will make all holiday preparations much easier.

This is a very simple project you can set up yourself with supplies you may have around the house or can find at a local office supply store.

You will need a twelve-page calendar for the current year. These can often be printed using a word processing program on your computer or purchasing one in an 8.5" x 11" format. A calendar will allow you to visually see the flow of the upcoming year and mark out  those days when you will not be available to get ready for the holidays because you have other commitments and pressures. This way you can plan some pacing for upcoming preparations. It will also allow you to designate launching and landing days for the especially important holidays that will demand considerable time and trouble to set up and take down.

No matter when the holidays happen during the week, most of your preparations would best be done by the end of the previous week. In addition, many of you will have children and/or other familial obligations that demand your immediate attention closer to the planned holiday. Preparing early means you can be respond better to the unknown events of life, which seem to frequently coincide with holiday celebrations.

An *Organized for the Holidays* binder is made by labeling the spine, front, and back with *Organized for the Holidays*. Put the twelve monthly calendars in the front of the binder.

Then purchase five binder tab dividers and label them:

- To Do

- To Give

- To Buy

- Decorate

- Entertain

Finally, put a sheet protector with a heavy piece of card stock, which has been labeled *Receipts,* in the back of your binder. You will also want sheets of lined paper upon which to do your planning and maybe even a pencil holder in the front of the binder for pens, pencils, post-it notes, and a calculator.

If you have money and the inclination, you might even add dividers for all the major holidays you face each year. This will allow you to keep specific notes about what worked and didn't work last time. Plus it will be a place for ideas and lists for the upcoming holiday celebrations.

I encourage you to get started on your holiday preparations by preparing your *Organized for the Holidays* binder, putting the calendars in front, purchasing and labeling the dividers, and getting everything all set up.

What will happen because of this preparation? Ideas will come to you about a creative way to celebrate your parents' upcoming 50th wedding anniversary and you can now make written notes. You will find a magazine description of a project you would like to do for Easter and now you have a place to keep it safe. A gift to get your husband this year for his birthday or maybe your father for Father's Day, or maybe the neighbors when they return from overseas will occur to you and you can now make a list of items to purchase.

You can now have one central place for all this information. When you begin to buy items, you have a place to put your receipts. And, when creative ideas come to mind in the middle of the night or the middle of dinner, you have a place to write them down.

So be sure to get your *Organized for the Holidays* binder up and functioning soon. If time is of an essence, you can purchase this binder at *www.houseoforder.com/products.htm.* Being organized for the holidays will make for a smoother and much more organized year.

40

Finish Up
and Move Forward

During the busy seasons in your life there are special needs.
This is especially evident the week before big events whether it
be a wedding, a graduation, or another festive occasion. When
the stress is high, I would like to suggest using the concept of
finish up and *move forward*.

You see, part of your preparations should be to finish up
routine chores and personal projects before the big event or
celebration's pressures officially begin to descend. There are
bills to pay, a little bit of deep cleaning to do here or there,
some projects you have been working on that would best be
brought to a partial finishing point and then put away until
sometime after the dust settles.

Another part of your preparations may be deciding what your
specific responsibilities will be for next week or so and moving
forward to get them done. If you will be traveling, you might
be making up of the list of things to take as you begin packing.
If you will be staying home and hosting company, it is time to
prepare a list of what items you need to purchase and the
projects to do each day until the big event has passed, including
your responsibilities for the *big* day.

Then, of course, you also have to plan for additional entertaining, shopping, and visiting if company is coming your way. Where will you go and what will you be doing together?

So as you prepare for a disruption to your regular routines, you should be focusing on both *finishing up* and *moving forward*. You will be going in two directions at once, one foot putting the brakes on and the other pushing the gas pedal. To prepare to both stop and start, walk around your house today with the pen and paper in hand and take notes. For example,

"I need to take care of that half-finished craft project."

"I had better put this vase away because our company includes younger children and I don't want it broken."

"I think I'll wrap this home improvement project up and put it away until after the celebration."

"I will clean the toilet a little bit better or our company will really notice the ring around the bowl."

"I will ...."

Then, after a tour of your home and a list of *finish up* items, sit down and make a *move forward* list. What needs to be done in preparation for the days ahead, what food need to be purchased, what arrangements still need formalizing, what people need contacting, and what decisions are still outstanding?

May your celebrations be more organized by focusing in two directions: *finishing up* and *moving forward*. Finish up everything that can be put away and plan for the things you will need to do for that big, upcoming festivity. Then celebrate!

41

Have Backup Plans

I am still learning the important lessons of backing up. You
see, just as a book I was writing was about to go to print, right
at the last moment on the last day, just as I was making the last
important changes, corrections, and improvements, my computer died (actually the fan on the motherboard quit, but it sure
sounded like a computer death). I hadn't backed up those files
for more than a week! Trouble. Real trouble.

Has this happened to you? Just when you need to drive a far
distance, you find the car empty of gas or a warning light
begins to blink? Just as you are walking out the door to an
important appointment, the phone rings with a potentially more
important call? Just as you think life is going along with some
sense of order, something or someone very important fails you.

If this continually happens to you, it is important to consider
the beauty, importance, and the absolute essential need for a
backup plan. If it rains, what will you do about your picnic? If
you have car trouble again, how will you get to the wedding on
time? If the reservation is cancelled, or the airplane doesn't
fly, or your ride doesn't pick you up, what will you do?

Just recently, one of my friends dropped a sibling off at the
airport, drove the two hours home only to discover a message
on the answering machine announcing the flight had been

cancelled because of turbulent weather. Back went my friend another two hours to pick up the sibling and then two hours back home again. The same scenario was repeated the second day, but this time my friend stayed until he was sure the airplane was in the air. What an expensive lesson!

As you go about the normal business of life, look at the bigger, upcoming events in your future and ask:

"If something fails or falters, what will I do? If it breaks, what will I do? If, just if, I need a backup, what can I do *now* so my backup plan will be in place?"

Once you have considered possible backup plans, notify the parties concerned and indicate what you will do if Plan A fails and you must proceed to Plan B. For instance, my friend now tells all his visitors he will be taking them to the airport, parking, and waiting with them until they are safely through security.

I now have a system to back up my computer files so I don't lose more than one hour or so of work. When I'm meeting a party in a faraway place, I always indicate that if something goes wrong and I won't be *here,* they can plan to find me *there.* If they can't contact me in this way, they can plan to contact me using this *phone number.* This mentality can save so much misunderstanding and often saves much time and emotional trauma.

"I will plan this way, but if something happens, I will plan on that way."

Of course, I am now backing up my computer files with regularity. I must remember not to eventually be lax and slothful. If it can fail, it probably will. If I am ready with a backup plan and have this plan in place, I will be glad for the beauty of backups!

42

A Thanks Bank Perspective

Even with adequate planning, there are some holidays that can cause you a lot of challenge. For instance, Thanksgiving can be one of the most stressful days of the year, especially if you are hosting a large crowd for dinner. How can you relieve the stress from this gratitude day or any holiday, for that matter? How about using the *Thanks Bank* concept?

After you get through the stresses of a holiday, prepare several lists that will help make this same holiday easier next year. Then bank them in your *Organized For the Holidays* binder where they can easily be retrieved and used during the next holiday to improve that holiday celebration.

For instance, at Thanksgiving this year, you might review this year's events, make written notes, and store them for use next

November. In a way you are putting these notes into a *Thanks Bank*. Having these lists will save you lots of trouble over the next several years. Four different lists are useful in preparation for Thanksgiving or any other major holiday or celebration.

One list should identify the items to do/purchase/find in order to be able to put on a nice Thanksgiving dinner. It includes things you need to buy at the store, items to retrieve from the storage room, and a reminder to purchase or find holiday napkins.

The second list has everything you need to do before Thursday like arrange the table centerpiece and polish the turkey platter. You might even make/buy several food items and put them away, as there might not be time on Thursday morning for such activities.

The last list is the things you will need to do on Thursday so the meal will be served on time, such as cut the bread into cubes for the dressing, put the olives in the frig, and check a second time that you have cranberry sauce (and any other items you tend to forget).

Also, make up a written list of cleanup projects to finish up the holiday after the company has said their goodbyes, your family has returned to regular routines, and you are facing the post-holiday cleanup. Use this list to note where you are putting the new Thanksgiving centerpiece and table runner so you can find them easily next year. You can make notes about changes you will incorporate next year including having a fun snack food project for the youngsters so they can be entertained and will not get so hungry before the big meal. You might also include foods you should prepare more of and those you can delete. For example, the layered jello salad was a hit, but too much work and everybody raved over the tiny sausages that disappeared too quickly.

So create your own *Thanks Bank* by preparing written notes, one with the list for the grocery store, one with a list of activities to do before the holiday, a list of things to do on the holiday, and finally a list of cleanup projects. Then your mind will be free to entertain the other stresses in your life during a holiday season, rather it be your spouse's pressures at work, the children's needs at school, or how to handle a particularly difficult guest graciously.

Remember, create your own *Thanks Bank* and you'll be more ready for successful holidays next year, including your particularly stressful ones, whether is be Thanksgiving, New Year's, or Mother's Day.

43

The Angel on Your Street

I met an angel recently. At least I think so. She is a woman in my neighborhood that became aware of some specific family needs in another town and thought she would do something about it this month. The husband had less than adequate employment, the pantry was rather bare, and the upcoming holidays looked somewhat bleak. She is no different than many others I have met through the years, but I was made glad because her requests helped me let go of things I really didn't need or want and yet hadn't had the courage to share. (I cling so tightly to my stuff.)

The requests were small: gently used clothing, unused canned goods, coats that were gathering dust, and toys that were no longer really being used.

As I went through my house, pulling cans from the pantry, finding a pair of shoes that really didn't work for me, and purging the unused board games, I felt cleaned out and re-freshed. I keep so much I really, really don't need, and actu-ally should share, but who will appreciate it enough to make the sharing worthwhile?

So, take just a few minutes and find the angel items in your house. Yes, give, give, give! It won't cost you a thing; it won't even dampen your style. In fact, it will help you get more organized and ready for the influx of more possessions that are surely to come your way soon enough.

So look for those angel items, gather them in a box or bag, and then look for an angel who is collecting items to share with others. You might even want to get your kids involved, maybe include your spouse, and definitely ask for contributions from your friend down the street that could use to lose a few items from her personal stash.

Find the order that returns to your home and heart when you have stripped yourself of what you don't really need. What a relief it is to give away what is useful but not needed any longer, especially when you give these treasures away to an angel!

44

Maintain Functional Chaos

During more complex holiday seasons of the year, you might have to move to a mode of functional chaos. Many of you will occasionally have a disruption in your regular routines during a holiday season. Sometimes this is all fun and good. At other times, it is just plain difficult.

But no matter the results, it is up to you to incorporate the concept of functional chaos into your priorities. This means that every morning during the holidays you are going to focus first on yourself. Get yourself prepared for the day before you emerge to meet the needs of your immediate family, guests, relatives, and friends.

This means doing whatever personal habits springboard you for a good day, like a bit of exercise, taking a hot shower, adding some lipstick, putting a brush through your beautiful hair, and wearing some bright, happy clothes!

Then, with yourself all in order, you can meet the needs of others. You might even have time to tackle the undone laundry, start the dishes that didn't get done after last night's snack, clean up the front room mess from a fun game of charades, and remove the muddy grime on your front porch in anticipation of more guests tonight.

May you enjoy the more hectic periods of life as you back off a rigorous routine and enjoy every gentle, unexpected experience. May you also find order in your personal life so you can function at your highest level. Remember, first you take care of you, then him/her (if you are so lucky to have one of these in your life), and then them. Keep yourself functional even though you know that it is likely to be a bit chaotic until regular routines return.

45

Catnap Craze

What if you made the catnap craze a part of your holiday season? You will probably have so much adrenaline flowing during the holiday season, what with extended family being around, eating delicious food, doing unaccustomed activities and staying up until crazy hours. You might need to add to your list to get a catnap once in awhile. It is a catnap craze because when things are settled down in your life, it is one of the last things you might ever think of doing.

But, during major holidays, it may help you keep going, keep you from getting sick, help you from losing it all together when you become grouchy, and otherwise make it possible for you to cope with having your children home from school, spending  the holidays with your in-laws, or even something as simple as having to clean up snow brought indoors after a fun afternoon with the children building a snowman.

When you get too tired to be useful, think about and work into your schedule a catnap here and there. Even fifteen minutes using a timer and laying quietly on your couch will work wonders. At other times, you might just go away into your bedroom for some time alone because even if you just lay still your body can rest and be renewed for the pressing needs of the rest of the day.

For example, if your teenage daughter shows up to help fix dinner, ask if you can steal away to a quiet bedroom and crash for a 15-minute nap. If your son volunteers to set the table, lay down while he mans the kitchen. If your spouse comes home early and offers to take over for a bit, find that bed. Taking these catnaps will make the holidays so much nicer and you will be a more pleasant person, too.

And don't forget to relax your schedule just a little bit in the morning if your spouse is off work, all the kids are home, and everyone is sleeping in. Sleep in yourself just a bit. Everyone knows that a rested person is better company than otherwise during the holiday season. Remember to catch the catnap craze and sneak a catnap once in a while so you can keep going through the entire chaotic frolic that comes with the unsettled schedule of the holidays. Happy catnapping!

46

The Day After

Just like you should organize for important events in your life, you must effectively prepare for the day after a big event in order to keep your pacing intact. Otherwise, you might lose control of the entire following week. If you plan on using several skills, the day after can go a little bit smoother.

Keep the day after free from any other major obligations. If you have a big party in your home on Tuesday, don't plan on doing other important projects on Wednesday because you will need extra time to finish up from Tuesday evening's gala. If others ask for your help, time, or energy, simply reply,

"I'm sorry. I already have another obligation on Wednesday. Maybe I could help another day."

Keep as much spare time as possible safe for your day after needs.

Even though you will do some cleaning up right after the event, plan even more time the day after to clean up and put away until things are back to normal.

Because the excitement of the celebration seems to stay in your heart into the next day (as it stays in the minds of others), there will likely be calls from those you hosted and calls to and from special friends who attended the event who will want to remember the good times together via phone. There will also need to be time to prepare your written thank you notes to those that brought refreshments or traveled a particularly long distance.

Finally, plan some time for being weary. Realize that on the day after you will probably be tired. You can handle the after-effects of the celebration and these fatigued feelings just a little better if you plan on being somewhat lethargic.

During any festive season of the year, there will be celebrations to anticipate, parties to plan, important events to attend, and social gatherings to host. In all these cases, you need to plan for the day after needs. There will be cleaning up, verbal and written thank yous, and a possible snooze, so keep the day after safe from other pressures and gently ease back into the main stream of life.

47

Shed and Share New Stuff

When it's past the big holiday gift giving season, its time to conquer all the new stuff. There are several great ways to bring order back to your life, especially regarding gifts.

After you have separated out those gifts that will be useful in your life, it is time to shed and share. Some gifts can go immediately into your gift box to give away again. The intent was nice and the gift welcome, but the gift's usefulness in your life is questionable. Giving it again is a great answer!

Other gifts are nice and useful enough, but they are in the wrong size, wrong color, or wrong brand. Put these together for the next trip to town. Put the gift receipt in the bag with each gift to facilitate returns. Plan on doing your returns earlier in the day as this will save dealing with larger crowds.

If the gift is useful and needed, find a home for it. Can it totally replace something you already have? If it is a duplicate tool or trinket, do you really need two? How about giving the old one away so the new will have more room and be easier to find?

There are gifts that are neither useful nor needed in your life. They are often sentimental gifts, lovely in their own way, but how many is enough? They are often also useful, but because they are not needed, well... If you don't really, really love it, let it go to make someone else happy.

You will have to decide how long you have to politically keep some items, but for the most part, let them go sooner than later. Alternatively, give something else away so your new gift guest has a nice home until you have the courage or the sufficient time needed to give it away again. I often put these items in my *Next Year's Holiday* gift box (because one year's wait is sufficient time to love a gift before sharing it again).

So after any special celebration, clean up the gift mess, deciding and sorting with a goal to keep the house just as ordered as before the festivities began. Put away, give away, or store away gifts to keep your life as uncluttered as possible.

ORGANIZED FOR TRAVELING AND MOVING

48

Your Motel Stay

Every time you travel, you learn how to travel wiser and smarter. Then, you can employ these important skills to make any motel stay a bit nicer, safer, and more comfortable.

For example, in my own travels, I have learned much. When making reservations, ask for an upper floor room, away from the stairwell, on the quiet side of the motel. This will make the initial walk to your room longer, but you will sleep with less noise and be less inter-rupted by the late night comings and early morning leavings of others.

Then, after you have opened your room and brought up your luggage, check that you have sufficient complimentary toiletries to make for a nice night's stay before you begin to settle in, get ready for your shower, and find that the shampoo or a goodly number of bath towels are missing.

It is also useful to bring a small night-light. Most motels seems to have the bathroom light switch attached to the fan, which makes midnight trips to the bathroom a family affair instead of a private one. A small night-light will give you or someone else what light is needed, just as much light as is needed, without the fanfare.

Keep a pen flashlight close at hand to help you find what you might need after all others have retired. This lets others sleep even while you are checking that your needs are close by where you can easily find them. This might be pain medication for an anticipated headache or a kleenex to handle hay fever sniffles. A miniature flashlight at your bedside helps makes your nighttime suitcase search quieter and more efficient.

Of course, traveling with your own pillow makes for a better night's sleep and a battery alarm clock keeps you independent, so these and other small trip tools will add to your comfort and the ease of your trip.

A rare treasure is a small roll of duct or clear moving tape. Use a piece of this to overlap the curtains sufficiently to make your room reasonably dark for sleeping. Otherwise that slit and the entering exterior light can keep you awake into the early morning hours and then awaken you before you are ready to arise.

Lastly, have a private stash of personalized toiletries, needs, and luxuries. Bring small containers and quantities, but if you use it regularly, bring it along. This might include your favorite crème rinse so your hair will be just right for the trip, perfume for that special evening extravaganza, and sharp scissors to trim your hair here and there.

After your stay and the repacking up of your vehicle, take a second, last look around the motel room before leaving. You might have everything of yours packed and in the car, but someone you love just might have overlooked his or her treasures. It is always better to double check now rather than double back later.

Traveling and motel staying can be fun, but it will also be more pleasant if you are prepared to stay your way with all of your needs. Happy traveling!

49

The Big Move

On occasion, I have helped others move across the country in a moving van, which we packed and unpacked ourselves. One car is often attached on a trailer behind the moving van and a second car follows loaded with additional personal items. There is a lot learned on such adventures, some ideas of which are worth sharing because past mistakes need not be repeated in your own packing and long-distance moving.

When packing, put as many items as possible in standardized boxes of three sizes: small, medium and large. Put heavy items in small boxes (such as books and paperwork), medium-weight items in mid-sized boxes (such as pans and kitchen utensils), and bulky, large items in oversized boxes (including lamp shades, bedding, pillows, and silk flower arrangements). Pack each box as full as possible and then put crushed newspaper, clothes or linens around the items until the box is completely full. This keeps each box from being crushed at the corners and also protects the contents.

Standard-sized boxes make it easier to load the truck because they can be readily stacked. Clearly mark lightweight and fragile boxes as you pack them. Set them aside for loading towards the last, as they should be stowed near the top of the truck or trailer to avoid being crushed by other, heavier items.

If you have fewer possessions, label the boxes on both ends with *STAY PACKED* (items of low importance) or *STAY OUT* (items of high importance). This will help you know what boxes are essential to initially set up your new abode into a friendly and useful home. It will also allow for more leisurely unpacking of less important items.

If you have many possessions and more family members, label each box with the room where it should be put once you arrive at your destination. This will facilitate getting the boxes in the right location for easy opening. This labeling when packing saves alot of time at the end of a long move.

Rent plenty of blankets from the moving company. These should be carefully put around, over, behind and in front of all furniture items that will touch each other. Otherwise, when you drive, the inevitable road bumps cause friction scars that are avoided with the judicious use of these moving blankets.

Rent a larger hand truck (with a strap). This will facilitate moving the bulky items up and/or down stairs and on and off the truck. Even if items won't go up the stairs easily on the hand truck, once these items have been hand carried to the right floor, they can be transported down halls and into rooms more readily with the hand truck.

Know your new home well enough so you can direct others (or know yourself) where to leave the floor empty for the mat-tresses (so you can get a good night's sleep if you don't get the bed frames made up the first night). Leave other floor areas empty to locate couches, pianos, end tables, and other bulky furniture near where their final location will be. That way, heavier items won't have to be moved twice.

With these moving tips incorporated into your next move, your companions will find you brilliant and you will feel much more contented until you are comfortably moved in.

50

Urban Camping
in a New Abode

Going urban camping is a unique opportunity. Now this
recreation may be new to some of you, so here are some of the
details. When you drive across the country in two vehicles,
staying at hotels and friends' homes along the way during a
three-day adventure, you suffer for none of the niceties of life
because these places are well stocked.

When you arrive at your destination and have unloaded the
truck, you will probably begin an urban camping trip. You
might be hot and sweaty from your labors. You might be
thirsty and hungry. You might even want to sleep comfortably
through the night. So you attempt to figure things out. Where
are the soap, shampoo, towels, and shower curtain? And if you
can find these essentials, how will you hang the curtain if no
shower curtain holders are to be found? These and other
immediate needs make for interesting urban camping adventures.

However, if you pack an *Essentials* box or two, the first night
of urban camping at your new location will easier to manage.
New apartments don't usually come with toilet paper, hand
soap, and paper cups, as you would find in a motel. Without

these essentials you have soiled hands, drink from the tap, and become somewhat desperate for a toilet paper substitute. So think about your everyday needs and pack a special, last on the truck box accordingly.

Even as you pack an *Essentials* box, you might consider a second box just for everyday tools to make the first day or two after your move so much nicer. Hammers, nails, screwdrivers, tapes of all kinds, rope, string and other tools will make it easier to go camping at your new home.

Also, if you are planning for a trip which would include overnight urban camping as you help someone move into a new abode, consider bringing the following in your suitcase: spare toilet paper (in case their toilet paper stash can't be found), a personal washcloth and towel, two flat sheets and a light blanket (so you'll be comfortable even if you're sleeping on the front room couch), shampoo in diminutive bottle, and a small bar of hand soap.

So if you want to order your life for occasional urban camping, consider what you will absolutely need to function and then stock, pack, and keep close at hand those tools and products that will make your unique camping trip just a bit nicer.

51

Finish the Move

Often, after you have initially moved into your new home, some moving projects are left undone. Sometimes it is unpacked boxes in the garage and/or closets stacked and neglected with their contents unused and gathering dust. Sometimes it is moving boxes that have not yet been retired. You have mostly moved in, but not quite and so those boxes sit unattended.

If you haven't looked in the unpacked boxes for a considerable period of time, should they be unpacked now and the items stored in your home, or instead, should they be taken to the thrift store? This is an interesting question and requires little thought because the answer is yes!

With the exception of family history items or other precious, sentimental treasures, if you haven't used these packed items, out they should go. Open each box, do a quick search through the contents, and if it isn't precious and/or you haven't needed it since you moved in, seriously consider closing the box right back up and sending it to the thrift store.

If empty moving boxes have been left around, they should also be addressed along with the crumpled newspaper, packing peanuts, or cardboard dividers they sometimes contain. While they are useful and might even be needed sooner than later, get the packing peanuts and paper into a large garbage bag, the boxes flattened, and all these items deep-stored or discarded. You don't need to feel like you are going to move again every time you enter the basement or garage just because you never finished moving in this last time.

Sometimes, you don't finish the move because you get distracted as those around you want to take up regular life again before the move has been finished. More often, you might become ill from the stress and cultural shock of the move and by the time you are back on your feet, you are behind without much chance to catch up on regular life, let alone finish the move.

It is now time to finish your last move, whether it took place six weeks, six months, or six years ago. With all the diligence you can muster, put off continuing your new life until you have finished moving in. Don't start any new projects until you have set up shop and are done with this last move. If that means taking boxes of useful, but unneeded items to the thrift store, so be it. Yes, you might want to open each of them to make sure that personal, embarrassing or useless items won't be donated, but no cheating. If you don't need it, you don't need it. Anonymously share it again with someone. You will never know where it goes, you will never see it used again, but neither will you be burdened with unfinished packing.

In the same way, if moving in means an afternoon in the garage slitting the tape on those great moving boxes and flattening them, it is time to get it done. Throw out the useless, bent or weak boxes. Get rid of packing materials that have shredded or disintegrated past usefulness. Finish, finish, finish!

So now it is time to complete this important project and set up shop. Everything will be different and better when you have settled in. If you don't like this place, wished you hadn't moved in the first place, and are even waiting for a chance to be gone, keeping the move half done won't help things a bit. You will be happier and things will work better if you are done.

So look around your house, storage areas, and garage. There are probably several unopened and unused boxes here or there from the last move. Find them, unpack and decide, and be done. It will be nice to finally be home and settled down.

ORGANIZED FOR THE FUTURE

st the many projects and problems on your mind, choosing
ose that will be put on hold when your stress increases and
ose that will need finishing or resolving soon. Decide what
ojects will just have to wait until this busy season has surren-
red to calmer days. With your weekly map in hand, your
any ventures can be addressed immediately or be safely
ved in writing until you can take them up again later.

is weekly map form can work beautifully for you, so much
 that you will probably make great progress on the first day
u use it. It will focus your energies on the items you have
ted, help you run errands with confidence because you know
at stops you will be making as you head towards home, and
at you will be doing when you have returned safely. You
ll also know what you have decided can and should wait
til later and so your mind can be at rest.

plicate the format on the following pages or download it
e from *www.houseoforder.com/downloads.htm.* Then your
n mind can dump out and you can begin to make more
derly sense during any busy time of your life. Remember,
u get a better grip with a written plan and can confidently
ve forward to have the greatest success!

52

Weekly Maps

Sometimes you might face a very busy season in life. There is too much to do with too little time to finish. There might be company to divert you from daily routines, a demanding familial situation, or even emergencies to keep you away from home. When your mind is otherwise occupied with these needs, use a simple weekly map/goal sheet (time schedule printed on one side and goals list printed on the reverse side) to keep yourself mentally intact while you tackle, prepare, entertain, or work your way through the *busy* season.

After preparing and printing a weekly map, sit for a bit and unload your mind onto this useful piece of paper. Ask yourself pertinent questions.

What will this next week bring? When do you need to be here and when do you need to be there? What errands do you need to run along with your other comings and goings?

When can you tuck in a project during some known empty time and another project during another waiting time? When could you be doing two things at once? Whom do you need to call? Where can you expedite your use of energy? What needs to be finished?

List the many projects and problems on your mind, choosing those that will be put on hold when your stress increases and those that will need finishing or resolving soon. Decide what projects will just have to wait until this busy season has surrendered to calmer days. With your weekly map in hand, your many ventures can be addressed immediately or be safely saved in writing until you can take them up again later.

This weekly map form can work beautifully for you, so much so that you will probably make great progress on the first day you use it. It will focus your energies on the items you have listed, help you run errands with confidence because you know what stops you will be making as you head towards home, and what you will be doing when you have returned safely. You will also know what you have decided can and should wait until later and so your mind can be at rest.

Duplicate the format on the following pages or download it free from *www.houseoforder.com/downloads.htm*. Then your own mind can dump out and you can begin to make more orderly sense during any busy time of your life. Remember, you get a better grip with a written plan and can confidently move forward to have the greatest success!

52

Weekly Maps

Sometimes you might face a very busy season in life. too much to do with too little time to finish. There m company to divert you from daily routines, a demand familial situation, or even emergencies to keep you a\ home. When your mind is otherwise occupied with tl needs, use a simple weekly map/goal sheet (time sche printed on one side and goals list printed on the revers keep yourself mentally intact while you tackle, prepar tain, or work your way through the *busy* season.

After preparing and printing a weekly map, sit for a bit unload your mind onto this useful piece of paper. Ask pertinent questions.

What will this next week bring? When do you need to and when do you need to be there? What errands do yo to run along with your other comings and goings?

When can you tuck in a project during some known em and another project during another waiting time? When you be doing two things at once? Whom do you need to Where can you expedite your use of energy? What need finished?

WEEKLY MAP

	Sun	Mon	Tues	Wed	Thurs	Fri	Sat
6:30							
7:00							
7:30							
8:00							
8:30							
9:00							
9:30							
10:00							
10:30							
11:00							
11:30							
12:00							
12:30							
1:00							
1:30							
2:00							
2:30							
3:00							
3:30							
4:00							
4:30							
5:00							
5:30							
6:00							
6:30							
7:00							
7:30							
8:00							
8:30							
9:00							
9:30							
10:00							
10:30							

	Daily goals	Current projects	Future projects	Weekly goals	Current projects	Future projects	Weekend plans
1							
2							
3							
4							
5							
6							
7							
8							
9							
10							

53

Map Out Twenty Years

One of the best ways you can organize for your future needs is to understand where you and/or your family are going to go over the next couple of decades. This is useful as you plan your life's goals, think about having children, contemplate their education needs, and look at the relationships you might anticipate. For example, using a twenty-year map, young parents with three children might realize that in five years they will have one daughter in junior high school, a son in elementary school, and a youngster still at home. In ten years they will have a daughter graduating from high school, a son in junior high school, and another daughter in elementary school. Other children might also have joined the family. Using the map to graphically see the probable dynamic changes in the family can help families anticipate various needs such as finances for education, employment opportunities to encourage independence in their growing children, and family vacations to enrich their traditions and memories.

Make your twenty-year map by drawing ten columns and ten rows on two clean sheets of papers, creating a form similar to the one on pages 152-153. You can also download the map free at *www.houseoforder.com/downloads.htm*.

1) Label the columns across the top row. The first column will be for the names of family members. The rest of

the columns will be for the years from now until twenty years from now, for example 2010 to 2029.

2) In the rows of the first column, list the names of individual family members. For example: Dad, Mom, Tom, David, Brian, Jenn, and Tyler.

3) Indicate in each appropriate box across their row the age each person will be during the year listed at the top of the sheet. A child born in 2005 will be five in 2010, ten in 2015, and etc.

4) Also, note in each appropriate box potential significant events in each person's life, such as when your children will enter elementary school, enter junior high, turn 16 and begin driving, enter high school, turn 19, graduate from high school and possibly enter college or voca-tional school. You might also speculate when they will likely graduate from college, consider marriage, etc.

5) Note the significant years in your own life. When will you be turning 30, 40, and 50? When will you likely have no one home during the day if you are a stay-at-home mom? When will you and your spouse be of re-tirement age?

6) Some families will want to include other important people, besides immediate family, in their map, like grandchildren. You may even want to extend your map to 25 or 30 years to show a broader spectrum.

Such mapping will show you the possible scenarios and vari-ous challenges, financial needs, and emotional strains as you and those you love mature together. It will give you a sam-pling of what you can expect as the years pass and help you understand the pressures that will come.

Most importantly, it will show you how few years there are between now and when your children might be leaving home for one reason or other. This gives impetus to the home training needed for your children and the nurturing needed for your grandchildren. I encourage you to make up a 20-year map. What will you and your family be doing over the next twenty years?

This organization time map helps you see what you can expect during the next two decades and helps you organize so you can be ready for your future, having taught them well and focused on what really mattered.

2 0 - Y E A R   M A P

	2010	2011	2012	2013	2014	2015	2016	2017	2018	2019
Name: Age										
Name: Age										
Name: Age										
Name: Age										
Name: Age										
Name: Age										
Name: Age										
Name: Age										
Name: Age										
Name: Age										
Name: Age										

2 0 - Y E A R   M A P

	2020	2021	2022	2023	2024	2025	2026	2027	2029
Age									
Name:									
Age									
Name:									
Age									
Name:									
Age									
Name:									
Age									
Name:									
Age									
Name:									
Age									
Name:									
Age									
Name:									

Endnote...

Remember, read this book to learn new principles, practice the skills you need most, and come back again and again to discover more.

Organization is always a process. You don't get organized and stay there. You work to be more organized. You strive to find better answers. You organize as you go. It has worked for me. I know it will work for you, too!

~ Marie

About Marie Ricks...

Marie has been sharing home organization skills for more than 20 years. In 1986, she began teaching an eight-week, sixteen-topic course at a local community center, which included classes on time management, food preparation, closet and cupboard organization, budgeting, teaching children to work, and shopping skills.

Marie's classes have proven popular both in San Jose, California and Utah County, Utah, where she now lives. Marie continues to teach home organization classes and seminars at church, professional, and community gatherings. She also spends time coaching homemakers their own homes and helping them learn to be more organized. Marie has seen a lot of dirty laundry, cluttered closets, and untidy paperwork, all of which is very exciting to her.

Marie is a presenter at Brigham Young University's Education Week. Her *House of Order Handbook* addresses the many facets of home management plus offers numerous worksheets to make running a home easier for any homemaker. Another book, *Project Organization, Quick and Easy Ways to Organize Your Life,* was published by Deseret Book and is available in local bookstores. Marie writes columns for several venues, has had her own radio show, and appears as a featured guest on TV and radio.

She has a large library of home management materials, endorses high quality housecleaning products, and shares a weekly email newsletter for interested women. Sign up at *www.houseoforder.com.*

Marie has been happily married to Jim Ricks for 37 years and together they are the parents of five sons. Tom is a Math Education professor at Louisiana State University, David is attending medical school at Ohio State University, Brian is a computer science doctoral candidate at Brigham Young University (and a new husband), and Tyler desires an animation degree at B.Y.U. Evan, their youngest son, passed away as a young child from leukemia.

Marie and her family live in Highland, Utah where she and her husband grow a vegetable and fruit garden as their summer hobby and share creative indoor projects together on colder days.

Also by Marie Ricks...

House of Order Handbook   200+ pages of easy-to-follow instructions for setting up and maintaining an orderly home. This trade paperback includes some 80+ worksheets to help organize your paperwork, finances, and shopping needs. It teaches principles that work!

***House of Order Handbook* CD**   80+ worksheets from the *House of Order Handbook* in .pdf file format for convenient reprinting on your home computer. It will make keeping organized a breeze as you complete each and every organization project.

Project Organization: Quick and Easy Ways to Organize Your Life   170+ pages of effective personal and home organization projects for home managers in all seasons of their lives.

Organized For A Mission   225-page book to help you organize wisely for an LDS mission. It addresses items to buy and take, smart clothes shopping, essential kits to prepare, financial needs to consider, proper packing techniques, and organization for a successful return. It is useful for both Elders and Sisters.

Master Menu Cookbook   50+ spiral bound pages of reliable and simple recipes to get your Master Menu working every day of the week.

Express Housecleaning Plan   This 32-card laminated packet lists the various rooms and responsibilities that need your housekeeping focus. Used in simple rotation, the ringed packet helps the home manager focus on one room/job at a time to complete simple routines in a timely manner.

***Stay-At-Home Housecleaning Plan* Packet & Dividers**   150+ index cards which detail important daily, weekly, and more complex housework projects to keep your house clean **plus** 21 laminated, cardstock dividers.

***Working Person's Housecleaning Plan* Packet & Dividers**   165+ index cards which detail essential housework projects in a sequential manner to accommodate the more chaotic life while keeping the house clean **plus** 21 laminated, cardstock dividers.

***Cleaning Standards* Cards**   Five 8.5" x 11" heavy-duty laminated sheets, printed on both sides, which detail the essentials needed to get household jobs done right (whether you want the rooms "fast" cleaned, first side, or "deep" cleaned, second side).

Tiny Tots Chore Charts These 15 *child-size* chore charts (attached together with two sturdy rings) detail using both words and pictures the simple, personal organization skills a young child needs to be independent.

Teaching Children to Work **Packet & Dividers** 150+ index cards detailing the vital housekeeping skills children and/or teenagers need to survive in the real world as independent adults **plus** 12 laminated, cardstock dividers.

Family Information Binder **Kit** One 1" view binder and 75+ useful printed forms for a family of eight to keep track of the important information needed to run a family.

Home Manager Filing System These twenty-four printed labels and file folders will aid you in keeping and finding important papers with ease! This is a great way to organize your personal paperwork and get going with your life!

Taming Money With Your Honey Binder **Kit** One 1" view binder with forms, binder dividers, and instructions that will help you find financial constancy, have peace in your family, and gain complete financial independence.

Organized For A Move Binder **Kit** One 1" view binder, 20 pages of instructions, and five binder dividers to jump-start you for organized packing, moving, and settling into your new abode.

Organized for the Holidays Binder **Kit** One 1" view binder with instructions, five laminated dividers, 34 forms, and a place for receipts, all to make for more organized holidays, this year and every year.

House of Order **Tutorial CDs** 25 three-minute home organization lessons in audio CD format for your easy and informative listening. Listen in your car—while you are waiting during soccer practice, piano lessons, and other down times—or at home.

Microfiber Mops and Cleaning Cloths Clean your house with the convenience of high-quality, durable microfiber mops and cleaning cloths of various sizes and styles.

Housecleaning Aprons and Tools Having the right tools makes housekeeping a nicer adventure. An apron with oversized pockets will help you collect treasures and trash as you move from room to room. Additional housecleaning tools will ease your way through daily routines. See *www.houseoforder.com* to order all of these items.